Chapter 1: Introduction to Software Design Patterns

Overview

Welcome to the exciting world of software engineering and design patterns! In this first chapter, we will provide you with a comprehensive introduction to software design patterns and their significance in the field of software engineering. From industry veterans to novice programmers, everyone can benefit from understanding and implementing design patterns in their software development process.Design patterns are simply recurring solutions to common problems in software design. They are a set of tried and tested techniques that have been used over the years by experienced developers to tackle common software design challenges. In this chapter, we will explore the importance and history of design patterns, and how they can improve the quality and maintainability of your code.

Importance

In today's fast-paced technology and business landscape, the demand for efficient and scalable software is ever-increasing. With tight project deadlines and limited resources, developers are constantly searching for ways to improve their code without sacrificing quality. This is where design patterns become invaluable. By utilizing design patterns, developers can save time and effort by avoiding the reinvention of the wheel. Instead, they can rely on proven techniques to solve common design problems, resulting in cleaner, more maintainable code. Additionally, design patterns promote consistency and standardization across different projects, making it easier for developers to collaborate and maintain each other's code.Moreover, design patterns can also improve the performance of your software. By utilizing well-established patterns, developers can optimize their code and make it more efficient, resulting in faster execution and better overall performance. This can be especially crucial in industries such as finance or healthcare, where even the slightest delay in processing large amounts of data can have serious consequences.

History

The concept of design patterns in software engineering was first introduced by Christopher Alexander, an architect, in his book "A Pattern Language: Towns, Buildings, Construction." In this book, Alexander described a set of common patterns that could be used to solve problems in architectural design. This idea was further developed by the "Gang of Four" (Erich Gamma, Richard Helm, Ralph Johnson, and John Vlissides) in their book "Design Patterns: Elements of Reusable Object-Oriented Software." Since then, design patterns have become an essential part of the software development industry. The Gang of Four patterns, also known as the "GoF" patterns, are considered the foundation of design patterns and are still widely used by developers today. Over time, more patterns have emerged, and today there are hundreds of design patterns available for developers to use. While design patterns were originally introduced in the context of object-oriented programming, they are applicable to a wide range of programming paradigms and languages. From web development to mobile applications, design patterns can be useful in almost every aspect of software development.

In conclusion, the importance of understanding and utilizing software design patterns cannot be overstated. With their ability to save time, improve code quality, and promote consistency, design patterns have become an essential aspect of modern software engineering. In the following chapters, we will dive deeper into different categories of design patterns and how they can be applied in real-world scenarios. So, let's continue our journey into the world of software design patterns!

Chapter 2: Creational Patterns

Singleton Pattern

In the world of software engineering, complexity and frequent changes are constant. Creating and managing instances of objects can become a daunting task, leading to errors and inefficiency. This is where the Singleton Pattern comes in - a design pattern that ensures a class has only one instance and provides a global point of access to it. The Singleton Pattern is widely used in situations where there is a need for a single, shared instance of a class. This is important in scenarios where there are limited resources available, but access to a specific object is required from different parts of the codebase. By restricting the class to have only one instance, the Singleton Pattern provides a centralized point of control, thereby managing the complexity of managing multiple instances. To implement the Singleton Pattern, the class is designed to have a private constructor and a static method to access the single instance. The first time this method is called, it will create an instance of the class if it does not already exist. Subsequent calls to this method will return the existing instance, ensuring there is only one instance of the class at all times. The Singleton Pattern has several advantages, including improved performance and efficient use of resources. As there is only one instance of the class, repeated construction and destruction of objects are avoided, reducing overhead and improving overall performance. It also helps in ensuring global access to the instance, enabling simpler and more effective code.However, like any design pattern, the Singleton Pattern also has some drawbacks. As there is only one instance of the class, there is no room for variation or customization. This makes it challenging to adapt the code to handle different scenarios or changing requirements. Additionally, dependency injection and testing can become problematic with the Singleton Pattern, as the single instance of the class cannot be easily replaced for testing purposes.

Factory Method Pattern

Creating objects is a fundamental aspect of software development. As the codebase grows, managing the creation of objects becomes a challenge, leading to complex and hard-to-maintain code. The Factory Method Pattern solves this problem by encapsulating the creation of objects and providing a method for creating them. The Factory Method Pattern is a creational pattern that provides a way to create objects without specifying the exact class of object that is to be created. This provides a way to decouple the client code from the specific classes being created, making the code more flexible and maintainable. It also allows for the creation of objects at runtime, providing a way to create different variations of an object without changing the client code. To implement the Factory Method Pattern, a factory class is created, responsible for creating objects of different classes based on a specified set of criteria. This factory class provides a single point of control for creating objects, thereby simplifying the creation process. One significant advantage of the Factory Method Pattern is its flexibility and adaptability. As the codebase grows, new classes can be added, and the factory method can be extended to create these new objects without affecting the existing code. This makes it easier to adapt the code to changing requirements and scenarios.However, the Factory Method Pattern may also introduce unnecessary complexity in simple projects. The creation of too many factories and methods for creating objects can lead to a bloated codebase, making it harder to maintain. Additionally, adding too many variations of objects can also make the codebase more complex and challenging to understand.

Abstract Factory Pattern

The Factory Method Pattern enables the creation of objects without specifying the exact class, but what if there are related objects that need to be created together? This is where the Abstract Factory Pattern comes in - a creational pattern that provides an interface for creating families of related or dependent objects without specifying their concrete classes. The Abstract Factory Pattern encapsulates a group of individual factories that have a common theme or goal. It provides a way to create multiple objects that work together without having to know the specific classes of these objects. This promotes loose coupling between the client code and the objects being created, making the code more maintainable. To implement the Abstract Factory Pattern, an abstract factory interface is defined, specifying the methods for creating the different objects. Each variation of this abstract factory represents a different family of related objects. Concrete implementations of these factories are then created, providing a way to create specific versions of these related objects. One significant advantage of the Abstract Factory Pattern is its ability to create families of related objects. This promotes consistency and ensures that all objects are compatible and work together seamlessly. Additionally, it also allows for the easy addition of new variations of objects without affecting the existing code.However, the Abstract Factory Pattern can be challenging to implement and may introduce complexity in simple projects. As it is designed to manage multiple families of objects, it may be overkill for smaller applications. Also, changing or adding new variations of objects can become cumbersome and require changes to multiple factory classes.

Cultivating Designs with Creational Patterns

In conclusion, creational patterns play a crucial role in software engineering by providing elegant solutions to managing complexity and maintaining code flexibility. The Singleton Pattern ensures that there is only one instance of a class, promoting efficient resource management and global access to the object. The Factory Method Pattern provides a way to create objects without specifying the exact classes, promoting code flexibility and adaptability. The Abstract Factory Pattern takes this a step further and allows for the creation of families of related objects, ensuring consistency and compatibility. By incorporating these creational patterns in our designs, we can cultivate cheerfulness, sophistication, and maintainability in our codebase.

Chapter 3: Software Design Patterns - Adapting, Decorating, and Facilitating

Software design patterns are essential elements in developing high-quality, efficient, and maintainable software. They are tried and tested solutions for recurring design problems that software engineers encounter in their work. In this chapter, we will explore three popular design patterns - the Adapter Pattern, Decorator Pattern, and Facade Pattern - and how they can be utilized in software engineering.

Adapter Pattern: Turning Incompatibility into Compatibility

Have you ever been in a situation where you have a perfect solution for a problem, but it's not compatible with the existing system? The Adapter Pattern comes to the rescue in such cases by adapting an incompatible interface into a compatible one. This pattern acts as a middleman between two interfaces, translating one into the other.The Adapter Pattern involves three main components - the adaptee, the adapter, and the target interface. The adaptee is the existing class or component that needs to be adapted, the adapter acts as the interface between the adaptee and the target interface, and the target interface is the new interface that the adaptee needs to be compatible with.Let's take an example of a music playing application that has a built-in music player. However, a new streaming service becomes popular, and the users demand the option to play music from this service through the application. The music player is the adaptee, the adapter acts as the interface between the existing music player and the streaming service, and the target interface is the new streaming service.

Decorator Pattern: Enhancing without altering

In software development, there is always a need for adding new features or functionalities to existing classes or objects without altering their structure. The Decorator Pattern allows us to do just that. It adds new behaviors or functionalities to an object at runtime without affecting the behavior of the existing object.The Decorator Pattern consists of four main components

- the component, the concrete component, the decorator, and the concrete decorator. The component is the existing class or object that we want to enhance, the concrete component is the specific implementation of the component, the decorator adds new features to the component, and the concrete decorator is the specific implementation of the decorator.For example, let's say we have a graphic design software that allows us to draw shapes, add colors, and edit them. However, we want to enhance this software by adding the ability to add special effects to these shapes. The shapes are the components, the concrete shapes are the specific implementation, the decorator adds the special effects, and the concrete decorator is the specific implementation of the decorator.

Facade Pattern: Simplifying the Complex

In software development, there are often complex subsystems with a large number of classes that can be overwhelming and time-consuming to understand and use. The Facade Pattern provides a simple interface to access these subsystems, thus simplifying the complexity.The Facade Pattern consists of two main components - the facade and the subsystem. The facade acts as a simplified interface to access the subsystem, and the subsystem is the collection of complex classes that work together to provide a specific functionality.For example, in a banking application, there could be a complex subsystem for handling transactions, user accounts, and security. Instead of accessing each of these classes separately, the application can use a facade that provides a simplified interface for performing these tasks.

Conclusion

The Adapter Pattern, Decorator Pattern, and Facade Pattern are just a few examples of the wide range of software design patterns available to software engineers. These patterns not only provide efficient solutions to design problems but also make it easier to maintain and understand complex systems. As a software engineer, it is essential to have a good grasp of these patterns and know when and how to use them in your projects. So, go ahead and explore more design patterns and enhance your software development skills.

Chapter 4: Behavioral Patterns

Observer Pattern

The Observer pattern is a valuable tool in the world of Software Engineering. It allows for a one-to-many relationship between objects, where a change in one object will notify and update all of its dependent objects. This is crucial for maintaining consistency and real-time communication in a complex system. At its core, the Observer pattern consists of two main elements: the subject and the observers. The subject is the object that maintains a list of observers and notifies them of any changes. The observers are the objects that are interested in the subject's state and receive updates when it changes. To better understand this pattern, let's use an example from the world of social media. Imagine you are a popular celebrity with millions of followers. Every time you post a new picture on Instagram, your followers are immediately notified. In this scenario, you are the subject and your followers are the observers. They are interested in your state (your latest post) and are notified as soon as it changes. Now, let's apply this to Software Engineering. One practical use of the Observer pattern is in event-driven systems. Let's say we have a user interface that displays real-time stock market data. We can use the Observer pattern to update the user interface every time a new stock price is received. This ensures that the user is always looking at the most current information.Another benefit of the Observer pattern is its flexibility. Since the observers are kept separate from the subject, we can easily add new observers or remove existing ones without affecting the subject's functionality. This makes the Observer pattern a great choice for dynamic systems where the number of observers may change frequently.

Strategy Pattern

In the world of Software Design Patterns, the Strategy pattern is one of the most versatile and powerful ones. It allows for the encapsulation and interchangeability of algorithms at runtime, making it a valuable tool for building flexible and extensible systems. The Strategy pattern is all about having different strategies (or algorithms) to solve a particular problem. These strategies are interchangeable, meaning we can easily switch from one to another without impacting the system's functionality. This is achieved by having a common interface for all strategies, ensuring that they all adhere to the same contract. Going back to our stock market example, let's say we want to have different algorithms for calculating stock prices. One algorithm may be based on historical data, while another may take into account real-time market trends. By using the Strategy pattern, we can easily switch between these algorithms without making any changes to the core functionality of our system.This pattern also promotes code reuse and maintainability. Instead of having to write and maintain multiple copies of code for different algorithms, we can encapsulate them into different strategies and reuse them whenever needed. This makes our code more organized, easier to maintain, and more adaptable to change.

Command Pattern

The Command pattern is a popular behavioral design pattern that encapsulates a request as an object, allowing for parameterization and decoupling of the requester from the receiver. This may sound complicated, but it's actually a very simple concept that can be extremely useful in certain situations. Let's use a real-life example to understand this pattern better. Imagine you are at a restaurant, and you want to order a meal. You give your order to the waiter, and he brings it to the kitchen, where it is executed. In this scenario, you are the requester, the waiter is the invoker, and the chef is the receiver. The order itself is the command being executed. Now, let's apply this to Software Engineering. In a system with a complex user interface, the Command pattern allows us to encapsulate user requests into objects, making them easy to manage and execute. For example, let's say our user interface has a button that performs an action when clicked. Instead of having to code the action directly into the button, we can encapsulate it into a command object. This not only decouples the button from the action but also allows us to easily add new actions without having to change any existing code. One of the most significant advantages of the Command pattern is its support for undo and redo operations. Since commands are encapsulated into objects, we can easily keep track of the history of commands and revert them if needed. This is particularly useful in applications where users may want to undo or redo their actions.

In conclusion, the Observer, Strategy, and Command patterns are valuable tools for building flexible, maintainable, and extensible software systems. They not only promote code reusability and maintainability but also help us cope with changing requirements in a more structured manner. As Software Engineers, it is essential to have a deep understanding of these patterns and know when and how to apply them in our designs.

Chapter 5: Model-View-Controller Pattern

Model-View-Controller (MVC) is a popular design pattern used in software engineering for creating user interfaces. It divides an application into three interconnected components – Model, View, and Controller. This separation of concerns allows for easier maintenance, scalability, and flexibility of the code.

Explanation

The Model-View-Controller pattern is based on the concept of separating the user interface (View) from the data (Model) and logical operations (Controller) that manipulate it. This allows for clean and maintainable code, as each component has a specific role to play and can be modified or replaced without affecting the others.The Model represents the data and business logic of an application. It encapsulates the data and provides methods for accessing and manipulating it. The View is responsible for the presentation of the data to the users. It receives input from the users and sends it to the Controller for processing. The Controller acts as an intermediary between the View and Model, handling user input and updating the Model accordingly.

Benefits

There are several benefits to implementing the Model-View-Controller pattern in software development:

1. Separation of Concerns:
The MVC pattern separates the different aspects of an application, ensuring that each component has its own responsibility. This makes the code more organized and easier to maintain.

2. Extensibility:
Due to the separation of concerns, adding new features or modifying existing ones becomes easier in MVC. Changes in one component do not affect the others, allowing for better scalability and flexibility.

3. Reusability:
The Model and Controller components can be reused in different View components, reducing the need for duplicate code and increasing efficiency.

4. Ease of Testing:
Testing becomes simpler in MVC as the different components can be tested separately, making it easier to pinpoint any bugs or errors.

5. Improved User Experience:
The MVC pattern allows for a clear separation between the presentation layer and the business logic, resulting in a more user-friendly and intuitive interface.

Implementation

To implement the Model-View-Controller pattern in software development, there are a few key principles to follow:

1. Identify the different components:
The first step is to identify the different components of an application and their respective roles - Model, View, and Controller.

2. Define the communication flow:
Determine how the components will interact with each other. This includes deciding which component is responsible for triggering actions and how they will communicate with each other.

3. Create separate classes for each component:
Each component should have its own class, with clearly defined responsibilities and methods.

4. Establish one-way communication:
The data flow should be unidirectional - from the Model to the View through the Controller. This ensures that each component has a clear purpose and avoids confusion.

5. Use interfaces:
Interfaces can be used to define methods that must be implemented by each

component, ensuring consistency and adherence to the MVC design pattern.

In conclusion, the Model-View-Controller pattern is a powerful tool for software engineers to create user-friendly and maintainable applications. It allows for a separation of concerns and promotes extensibility, reusability, ease of testing, and an improved user experience. By following the principles and guidelines outlined above, developers can successfully implement MVC in their projects and reap its benefits.

Chapter 6: Model-View-Presenter Pattern

Differences from MVC

The Model-View-Presenter (MVP) pattern is a derivative of the popular Model-View-Controller (MVC) pattern, and is designed to address some of its limitations. In MVC, the controller acts as an intermediary between the view and the model, handling user interactions and data manipulation. This can lead to bloated and tightly coupled controllers, making it difficult to test and maintain. In MVP, the presenter takes on the role of the controller, serving as the middleman between the view and the model. The view is then responsible for purely displaying data, while the model handles the business logic and data storage. This separation of concerns allows for a cleaner and more efficient codebase, making debugging and updates easier.Another key difference is the way data is communicated between the layers. In MVC, the controller sets the data for the view to display, but in MVP, the presenter directly updates the view with the model's data. This reduces the number of dependencies and makes the code more easily testable.

Example Usage

To better understand how the MVP pattern is used, let's take the example of a shopping cart feature in an e-commerce website. In MVC, the controller would handle all interactions with the cart, including adding and removing items. However, in MVP, the presenter would handle these interactions by updating the view with the new cart information, while the model would handle the actual data storage.This allows for a more flexible and reusable codebase, as the presenter can be used for multiple views that require the same functionality, without having to duplicate code. Additionally, as the presenter is responsible for data updates, new features can be added without impacting the views, making it easier to scale the application.

Pros and Cons

Like any design pattern, the MVP has its own set of advantages and drawbacks. One of the main benefits of MVP is its ability to facilitate clean, modularized code, making it easier to maintain and update. As the code is separated into distinct layers, it also becomes easier to test, reducing the likelihood of bugs and errors. Another advantage is the improved user experience. As the logic and functionality are handled by the presenter, the view does not have to handle any data manipulation, resulting in faster and more responsive user interactions. Additionally, the separation of concerns in MVP makes it easier for developers to work on different parts of the codebase without interfering with one another. On the other hand, one of the main drawbacks of MVP is the increased complexity compared to MVC. While it may lead to a more efficient codebase, it can also require more time and effort to implement. Additionally, beginners may struggle to understand the different layers and how they interact with each other. Another potential issue is the lack of well-defined guidelines for implementing MVP. As the pattern is still relatively new, there is no standard way of structuring the codebase, which can lead to inconsistencies and confusion among team members.Nevertheless, with proper planning and implementation, the MVP pattern can greatly improve the structure and functionality of a software project. Its ability to enable code reuse, enhance user experience, and promote maintainability make it a viable option for modern software development.

Conclusion

In this chapter, we explored the Model-View-Presenter pattern and its differences from the traditional Model-View-Controller pattern. We looked at an example usage in a shopping cart feature and discussed the pros and cons of using MVP. While it may have some drawbacks, the MVP pattern offers a more modern and efficient approach to software design, making it a valuable addition to any developer's toolkit.

Chapter 7: Model-View-ViewModel Pattern

Explanation

The Model-View-ViewModel (MVVM) pattern is a software design pattern that is used in the development of user interfaces. It is based on the Model-View-Controller (MVC) pattern, but with some key differences. MVVM is widely used in front-end and cross-platform development, and is often the preferred architecture for mobile applications.At its core, the MVVM pattern separates the user interface (View) from the business logic and data (Model) using a mediator called the ViewModel. This allows for a clean and organized structure that makes it easier for developers to manage and modify their code.

Data Binding

One of the key features of the MVVM pattern is data binding. Data binding is a technique that allows for the automatic synchronization of data between the View and ViewModel. This means that changes made in the View will automatically be reflected in the ViewModel and vice versa. This not only reduces the amount of code needed, but also increases the efficiency and maintainability of the application.In MVVM, data binding is achieved through a powerful feature called Observables. Observables are objects that notify their changes to subscribers. This allows for real-time updates of data in the ViewModel and ensures that the View is always in sync.

Advantages

The MVVM pattern offers a number of advantages that make it a popular choice among developers. Some of these include:

- Separation of concerns: With MVVM, the code is divided into three distinct layers, each with their own responsibilities. This makes the code easier to understand and maintain.

- Testability: The MVVM pattern makes it easier to test the ViewModel and its business logic independently from the View. This allows for more efficient and comprehensive unit testing.

- Scalability: MVVM is a highly scalable architecture that can be easily extended to support new features and functionalities without affecting the existing codebase.

- Cross-platform compatibility: Since MVVM is independent of the user interface, it can be easily adapted for different platforms such as web, mobile, or desktop applications.

- Code reusability: With the help of data binding and observables, developers can reuse the same code logic for multiple views, reducing the amount of redundant code in the application.

In addition to these technical advantages, the MVVM pattern also promotes a more efficient and collaborative development process. With a clear separation of concerns, multiple developers can work on different layers of the codebase without stepping on each other's toes. This promotes a faster and more efficient workflow, resulting in a higher quality final product.

In Conclusion

The Model-View-ViewModel pattern is a highly efficient and popular architecture for building user interfaces. With its clear separation of concerns, data binding using observables, and cross-platform compatibility, it offers a number of advantages for both developers and end-users. Whether you are building a web application, a mobile app, or a desktop software, MVVM is a reliable and scalable pattern that can help you create a sleek and user-friendly interface. It's no wonder that MVVM is the preferred design pattern for many software engineers in the field of front-end development.

Chapter 8: Adapter Pattern

Explanation

The Adapter Pattern is a commonly used design pattern in software engineering that allows two incompatible or unrelated interfaces to work together seamlessly by acting as a translator between them. It is often used when trying to integrate legacy code with new code or when working with third-party libraries that have a different interface than what is needed for the current project. By using the Adapter Pattern, different components can communicate and interact with each other without having to change their code.

Use Cases

The Adapter Pattern is useful in many different scenarios where there is a need for integration between various components with different interfaces. For example, imagine a scenario where a company has an outdated system that they want to replace with a new one. The new system is built using modern technologies and has a different interface than the old one. Instead of rewriting the entire system, the Adapter Pattern can be used to bridge the two interfaces and allow them to communicate with each other seamlessly.Another common use case for the Adapter Pattern is when working with third-party libraries. Many times, these libraries have their own way of doing things and do not match with the rest of the codebase. In such cases, using the Adapter Pattern allows for a smooth integration without having to change the existing code.

Example Implementation

To better understand how the Adapter Pattern works, let's take a look at an example implementation. Imagine a music player that plays audio files of different formats such as MP3, WAV, and FLAC. The music player has a method called "play" that takes in the file name and plays the corresponding audio file. However, the music player can only play MP3 files, and we want to extend its functionality to play WAV and FLAC files as well.To achieve this, we can create an adapter class for each audio file format. These adapter classes will implement the same interface as the music player and internally use a third-party library to handle the conversion from the respective format to MP3. This way, when the "play" method is called, the adapter class will take care of converting the file to MP3 and passing it to the music player for playback.This implementation of the Adapter Pattern allows for the seamless integration of different audio formats with the music player without having to make any significant changes to the existing codebase.

Benefits of Using the Adapter Pattern

The Adapter Pattern offers several benefits, making it a popular choice among software engineers. Some of these benefits include:

1. Allows for code reusability: By using the Adapter Pattern, we can easily integrate legacy code with new code without having to rewrite the entire system.

2. Enhances flexibility: The Adapter Pattern allows for the addition of new components or functionality without affecting the existing codebase. This makes it easier to scale and maintain the system in the long run.

3. Promotes interoperability: Different components with different interfaces can work together seamlessly by using the Adapter Pattern, promoting interoperability and collaboration between them.

4. Simplifies integration: The Adapter Pattern simplifies the integration process by acting as a middleman between incompatible interfaces. This helps save time and effort in the integration process.

Conclusion

In conclusion, the Adapter Pattern is a powerful tool in the software engineer's arsenal that allows for seamless integration and communication between different components with different interfaces. It offers several benefits, including code reusability, scalability, and flexibility, making it a popular choice for achieving integration in software development. The use cases for the Adapter Pattern are endless, and it has greatly simplified the process of integrating legacy code with new code and third-party libraries. So, next time you encounter a situation where you need to bridge two incompatible interfaces, consider using the Adapter Pattern and see the magic happen!

Chapter 9: The Builder Pattern

The Builder Pattern is a creational design pattern that allows for the construction of complex objects in a step-by-step manner. This pattern separates the creation of an object from its representation, allowing for more flexibility and control over the construction process. In this chapter, we will explore the purpose, implementation, pros and cons of using the Builder Pattern in software engineering.

Purpose

The main purpose of the Builder Pattern is to simplify the creation of complex objects by breaking down the construction process into smaller, more manageable steps. This is especially useful when dealing with objects that have multiple attributes and configurations, as it can become overwhelming and error-prone to try and set all the values directly in the object's constructor. The Builder Pattern allows for a more structured approach to building objects, making the code more manageable and easier to maintain.

Implementation

To implement the Builder Pattern, we first need to define a builder class that is responsible for constructing the desired object. This builder class will have methods for setting each attribute of the object, and a final build method that will return the fully constructed object. The target object will also need to have a constructor that takes in the desired attributes as parameters. Let's take a simple example of building a car object using the Builder Pattern. Our builder class, named CarBuilder, will have methods for setting the car's make, model, color, and engine size. The Car class will have a constructor that takes in these attributes as parameters. In the builder's build method, we can call the Car constructor and pass in the values that were set through the builder's methods. This will return a fully constructed car object. One of the main advantages of using the Builder Pattern is the ability to chain its methods together. This allows for a more concise and readable code, as shown in the example below: Car car = new CarBuilder() .setMake("Tesla") .setModel("Model 3") .setColor("Red") .setEngineSize(2.0) .build();

Pros and Cons

As with any design pattern, there are both pros and cons to using the Builder Pattern. Let's discuss them in detail below.

Pros:

Flexible object creation:

Using the Builder Pattern allows for a more flexible object creation process. With the ability to set different attributes at different times, we can create objects with varying configurations without having to create multiple constructors or clutter the object's main constructor.

Readable code:

By separating the construction process into smaller, manageable steps, the code becomes more readable and self-explanatory. This makes it easier for other developers to understand the object's construction and to make changes if needed.

Dynamic creation of objects:

The Builder Pattern allows for dynamic creation of objects, meaning that the values of attributes can be changed at runtime. This is particularly useful when dealing with complex objects with many different configurations.

Cons:

Increased code complexity:

Implementing the Builder Pattern can add complexity to the codebase. With the addition of a builder class and multiple methods for setting attributes, the code can become more cluttered and less straightforward.

Requires additional classes and objects:

To implement the Builder Pattern, we need to create a builder class and possibly additional objects for each target object. This can lead to an increase in the number of classes in the codebase, which may not be ideal for smaller projects.

Not suitable for objects with few attributes:

The Builder Pattern is most useful when dealing with complex objects that have multiple attributes and configurations. For objects with only a few attributes, using the Builder Pattern may be unnecessary and may add unnecessary complexity.

In conclusion, the Builder Pattern is a powerful tool for simplifying the creation of complex objects in software engineering. With its structured approach and flexibility, it can greatly improve the readability and maintainability of code. However, like any design pattern, it is important to consider the pros and cons and assess if it is the right fit for the project at hand.

Chapter 10: The Beauty of the Prototype Pattern

The world of software engineering is constantly evolving, with new technologies and techniques emerging every day. And with this never-ending growth and development comes the need for efficient and effective design patterns to streamline the software development process. One such pattern that has gained widespread recognition and adoption in recent years is the Prototype Pattern. So, let's delve deeper into this elegant pattern and discover its intricacies and benefits.

Definition

At its core, the Prototype Pattern is a creational design pattern that allows developers to create new objects by cloning existing ones, thus avoiding the need to create new objects from scratch. Simply put, it involves creating an initial object, or prototype, and then creating new objects by copying and altering that prototype. This approach not only saves time and effort but also helps in maintaining a consistent and error-free software design.

Differences from Singleton

While the Prototype Pattern may sound similar to the Singleton Pattern, it is important to understand the key differences between the two. While both patterns involve creating objects, the Prototype Pattern allows for the creation of multiple objects from a single prototype, whereas the Singleton Pattern restricts the creation of only one object. Additionally, the Prototype Pattern allows for more flexibility as the prototype can be altered or modified to create different variations of the same object, while the Singleton Pattern does not allow for any modifications.

Example Usage

To better understand the practical applications of the Prototype Pattern, let's consider an example of a software that generates reports for a company. In this scenario, the prototype could be a pre-existing report template with a basic layout and design. From this prototype, the software can create new reports by cloning the prototype and then customizing it with specific data and information for each report. Not only does this save time and effort, but it also ensures consistency in report design.Another common application of the Prototype Pattern is in video game development. Many game engines use this pattern to create and display multiple characters on the screen. They use a base character as the prototype and then clone and customize it to create different characters with unique attributes and abilities.

The Art of Prototyping

Beyond its technical benefits, the Prototype Pattern also allows for more artistic freedom in software design. As developers are not limited to starting from scratch, they can experiment and play with different variations and prototypes before deciding on the final product. This can lead to more innovative and creative solutions that may have otherwise been missed.Moreover, the Prototype Pattern encourages a culture of collaboration and knowledge sharing among team members. By reusing and modifying existing prototypes, team members can build upon each other's work and improve the overall quality and efficiency of the software development process.

Cultured Efficiency

One of the key reasons for the popularity of the Prototype Pattern is its ability to streamline the software development process and increase efficiency. By reusing existing prototypes, developers can save time and effort, thus increasing productivity. Moreover, the consistent and error-free design that comes with using prototypes can help improve the overall quality of the software.Another advantage of the Prototype Pattern is its adaptability. As mentioned earlier, prototypes can be easily modified or customized to create different variations of the same object. This not only saves time but also adds to the aesthetic appeal and user-friendliness of the software.

Final Thoughts

In a constantly evolving industry like software engineering, having a reliable and efficient design pattern can make a world of difference. The Prototype Pattern not only saves time and effort but also encourages creativity and collaboration among team members. With its many benefits and widespread adoption, it is clear that the Prototype Pattern is here to stay and will continue to play a vital role in the design and development of software applications.

Chapter 11: Singleton Pattern

Explanation

Software design patterns are recurring solutions to common design problems that have been proven effective over time. One such pattern is the Singleton pattern, which is used to ensure that only one instance of a class exists in a system. This pattern is widely used in various programming languages, including Java, C++, and Python. In this chapter, we will explore the Singleton pattern in detail, its implementation, and the benefits it provides to a software system.

Implementation

The Singleton pattern is a creational pattern, meaning that it is used to create objects. Its main purpose is to control the creation of instances of a particular class, ensuring that only one instance is ever created and providing global access to that instance. There are various ways to implement the Singleton pattern, but the most common approach is using a private constructor, a static variable, and a static method to control access to the instance of the class. Let's take a look at a Java example of implementing the Singleton pattern: ``` public class MySingleton { private static MySingleton instance; private MySingleton() {} public static MySingleton getInstance() { if(instance == null) { instance = new MySingleton(); } return instance; } } ``` In this example, we have a private constructor, which means that the class cannot be instantiated from outside the class. We also have a static variable named "instance," which will hold the single instance of the class. The static method "getInstance()" is used to access the instance of the class. It first checks if the instance is null, and if it is, it creates a new instance and returns it. If the instance already exists, it simply returns the existing instance.

Benefits

Now that we have seen how the Singleton pattern is implemented, let's explore the benefits it provides to a software system.

1. Control over Object Creation:
The Singleton pattern ensures that only one instance of a class exists in a system, allowing for global access to that instance. This control over object creation can be useful in various scenarios, such as managing database connections or limiting the number of open files in an operating system.

2. Global Access:
By using the Singleton pattern, the instance of the class can be accessed globally from anywhere in the codebase. This eliminates the need to pass the object around or maintain multiple instances of the same class.

3. Thread Safety:
In multi-threaded environments, it is essential to ensure that only one instance of the class is ever created. The Singleton pattern ensures thread safety by providing a synchronized getInstance() method, which means that only one thread can access it at a time, preventing multiple instances from being created.

4. Memory Management:
In systems with limited resources, the Singleton pattern can be beneficial as it only creates one instance of the class and provides global access, reducing the memory usage and improving the overall performance of the system.

5. Easy to Change:
In case the requirements change, and there is a need for multiple instances of the class, the Singleton pattern can easily be adapted to create multiple instances instead of a single one. This makes it a flexible solution for managing object creation in a system.

Conclusion

The Singleton pattern is a powerful design pattern that provides control over object creation and global access to a single instance of a class. Its implementation is relatively simple, making it a popular choice among software developers. When used correctly, the Singleton pattern can contribute to creating efficient, scalable, and easily maintainable software systems.

Chapter 12: Factory Method Pattern

Software design patterns are an essential element in the field of software engineering. They act as a guide, providing developers with templates and solutions to common problems that arise during the software development process. One such pattern is the Factory Method Pattern, which falls under the category of Creational Patterns. In this chapter, we will dive deeper into the Factory Method Pattern, exploring its definition, implementation, and use cases.

Definition

The Factory Method Pattern is a creational design pattern that provides a standard interface for creating objects of a certain class, but allows subclasses to alter the type of objects that will be created. In simpler terms, it encapsulates the creation of objects, eliminating the need for the client code to specify the exact class of the object that needs to be created. This results in more flexible and loosely coupled code, as the client no longer needs to be aware of the implementation details of the object being created.The key elements of the Factory Method Pattern are the factory class, product interface, and product classes. The factory class is responsible for creating the objects, which are defined by the product interface. The product interface serves as the blueprint for the different types of objects that can be created, and the product classes are the concrete implementations of the product interface.

Implementation

To implement the Factory Method Pattern, the first step is to create an interface for the products that will be created. Then, concrete classes that implement this interface can be created. Next, a factory class is created with a method that returns an object of the product interface type. This method can also be made abstract, allowing the subclasses to provide their own implementations. Finally, the client code can use the factory method to create objects without having to specify the exact class of the object.Let's take a look at a simple example of implementing the Factory Method Pattern in Java. We will create a Shape interface, which will serve as our product interface. Then, we will create three concrete classes - Circle, Square, and Triangle -

that implement the Shape interface. Next, we will create a ShapeFactory class with a method called getShape(), which will return an instance of a Shape object based on the input given by the client code.

Shape.java

```
public interface Shape { void draw(); }
```

Circle.java

```
public class Circle implements Shape { @Override public
void draw() { System.out.println("Drawing a circle!"); } }
```

Square.java

```
public class Square implements Shape { @Override public
void draw() { System.out.println("Drawing a square!"); } }
```

Triangle.java
```
public class Triangle implements Shape { @Override public
void draw() { System.out.println("Drawing a triangle!"); }
}
```

ShapeFactory.java

```
public class ShapeFactory {

    public Shape getShape(String shapeType) {

        if(shapeType == null) { return null; }
        if(shapeType.equalsIgnoreCase("Circle")) { return
        new Circle();
        } else if(shapeType.equalsIgnoreCase("Square")) {
        return new Square();
        } else if(shapeType.equalsIgnoreCase("Triangle"))
        {
        return new Triangle();
        } return null;

    }
}
```

Now, in our client code, we can simply use the ShapeFactory to create a specific shape without needing to know about the implementation details.

```
public static void main(String[] args) { ShapeFactory
factory = new ShapeFactory(); Shape circle =
factory.getShape("Circle"); circle.draw(); }
```

Use Cases

The Factory Method Pattern has several use cases, including:

- When a class does not know which type of objects it will need to create
- When a class wants its subclasses to specify the objects it creates
- When a class wants to decouple its creations from the code that uses these objects

One of the most popular use cases of the Factory Method Pattern is in dependency injection frameworks, where the factory class is responsible for creating instances of objects to be injected into other classes.Another use case is in GUI programming, where the factory class can be used to create different widgets depending on user input or other conditions.

Conclusion

In conclusion, the Factory Method Pattern is a powerful tool that helps in creating flexible and loosely coupled code. It allows for easier maintenance, as any changes made to the product classes or interfaces will not affect the client code. It also promotes code reuse, as new product classes can easily be added without changing the client code. Consider using the Factory Method Pattern in your next software development project to improve the structure and maintainability of your code.

Chapter 13: Abstract Factory Pattern

Explanation

The abstract factory pattern is a creational design pattern that focuses on creating families of related objects without specifying their concrete classes. It is designed to encapsulate the process of object creation and provide a common interface for creating objects of related classes. This allows for the creation of different types of objects while maintaining a consistent structure and interface.The abstract factory pattern follows the principle of "programming to an interface, not an implementation". This means that the client code does not need to know the specific classes of the objects it is creating, but rather relies on the common interface provided by the abstract factory. This results in a more flexible and maintainable code, as changes to the concrete classes can be made without impacting the client code.

Structure

The abstract factory pattern consists of four main components: abstract factory, concrete factory, abstract product, and concrete product.

- Abstract Factory: This is the main interface that declares the methods for creating objects. It serves as a factory for creating families of related products.

- Concrete Factory: This is the implementation of the abstract factory interface. It creates specific instances of the products.

- Abstract Product: This is the common interface for the products created by the abstract factory. It is usually an abstract class or interface that defines the methods and properties that the concrete products must have.

- Concrete Product: These are the classes that implement the abstract product interface. They are created by the concrete factory and represent the different variations of the products.The following UML diagram illustrates the structure of the abstract factory pattern:

Real-world Examples

One real-world example of the abstract factory pattern is a car manufacturing plant. The plant produces different types of cars, such as sedans, SUV, and sports cars. Each type of car has its own set of parts, including engine, body, wheels, etc. The plant can be seen as the abstract factory, while the sedan factory, SUV factory, and sports car factory can be seen as concrete factories. The cars themselves represent the concrete products of the factory. Another example is a pizza restaurant that offers a variety of pizzas, such as New York-style, Chicago-style, and Neapolitan-style. The restaurant can be seen as the abstract factory, while the different types of pizzas represent the concrete products.In both these examples, the main benefit of using the abstract factory pattern is that it allows for the creation of different types of related objects without the need for the client code to know the specific classes of those objects. This makes the code more flexible and easier to maintain.

Conclusion

The abstract factory pattern is a useful tool for creating families of related objects in a flexible and maintainable way. It promotes loose coupling and follows the principle of "program to an interface, not an implementation". By using the abstract factory pattern, we can easily add or remove different types of objects without impacting the client code, making it a powerful technique in the world of software engineering.

Chapter 14: Decorator Pattern

The decorator pattern is a popular design pattern in software engineering that allows for the dynamic addition of new behavior to an object without changing its existing functionality. This pattern follows the principle of open-closed design, which states that classes should be open for extension but closed for modification. In this chapter, we will explore the decorator pattern, its benefits, and provide a code example to demonstrate its implementation.

Explanation

The decorator pattern is a structural pattern that allows developers to add new functionality to an existing codebase without modifying the original code. It involves wrapping an object in a decorator class that implements the same interface as the original object. This decorator class adds new behavior to the original object by delegating the calls to the underlying object and then adding its own functionality. This allows for the addition of multiple decorators, each adding a specific behavior to the original object.The decorator pattern is based on the concept of composition over inheritance, meaning that it is better to use object composition instead of class inheritance to achieve code reuse. With inheritance, classes can become tightly coupled, making it difficult to extend or modify code. However, with the decorator pattern, new functionality can be added in a flexible and efficient manner without altering the original codebase.

Benefits

There are several benefits of using the decorator pattern in software development. Some of the key advantages include:

- Flexibility:
The decorator pattern allows for the dynamic addition of new behavior to an object at runtime. This means that new functionality can be added without the need for changing the existing code, making it a flexible approach for code modification.

- Code Reuse:
The decorator pattern promotes code reuse by allowing developers to add new behavior to an object without modifying the original code.

- Scalability:
As the decorator pattern follows the principle of open-closed design, it results in code that is scalable and easily maintainable. New behaviors can be added by creating new decorator classes, and existing behaviors can be modified or removed by creating specific decorator classes.

- Separation of Concerns:
The decorator pattern separates the concerns of adding new functionality and modifying existing ones. This ensures that code is well-organized and easier to manage.

Code Example

To better understand the decorator pattern, let's take a look at a simple code example. Say we have a coffee shop that offers different types of coffee, such as espresso, latte, and cappuccino. Each coffee type has its own price and ingredients. Let's create a Coffee interface with two methods, getPrice() and getIngredients(), that will be implemented by all coffee types.

```
public interface Coffee { double getPrice(); String
getIngredients(); }
```

Next, let's create three coffee classes to represent our three different coffee types.

```
public class Espresso implements Coffee {

    @Override public double getPrice() {
        return 3.50;
    }
    @Override public String getIngredients() {
        return "Espresso";
    }
}
public class Latte implements Coffee {
    @Override public double getPrice() {
        return 4.50;
    }
    @Override public String getIngredients() {
        return "Espresso, steamed milk, and foam";
    }
}
public class Cappuccino implements Coffee {
    @Override public double getPrice() {
        return 5;
    }
    @Override public String getIngredients() {
        return "Espresso, steamed milk, and foam";
    }

}
```

Now, let's say we want to add additional ingredients to our coffee types, such as whipped cream or caramel syrup. Instead of modifying the existing classes, we can use the decorator pattern to add these behaviors dynamically. First, we will create an abstract class called CoffeeDecorator, which will implement the Coffee interface and serve as the base class for all decorators.

```
```

public abstract class CoffeeDecorator implements Coffee {
    private final Coffee decoratedCoffee;
    public CoffeeDecorator(Coffee decoratedCoffee) {
        this.decoratedCoffee = decoratedCoffee;
    }
    @Override public double getPrice() {
        return decoratedCoffee.getPrice();
    }
    @Override public String getIngredients() {
        return decoratedCoffee.getIngredients();
    }
}

```
```
```

Next, we can create specific decorator classes for each additional ingredient we want to add, such as WhippedCreamDecorator and CaramelSyrupDecorator.

```
```

public class WhippedCreamDecorator extends CoffeeDecorator {
    public WhippedCreamDecorator(Coffee decoratedCoffee) {
        super(decoratedCoffee);
    }
    @Override public double getPrice() {
        return super.getPrice() + 1.50;
    }
    @Override public String getIngredients() {
        return super.getIngredients() + ", whipped cream";
    }
}
public class CaramelSyrupDecorator extends CoffeeDecorator {
    public CaramelSyrupDecorator(Coffee decoratedCoffee) {
        super(decoratedCoffee);
    }
    @Override public double getPrice() {
        return super.getPrice() + 2;
    }
    @Override public String getIngredients() {
        return super.getIngredients() + ", caramel syrup";
    }
}
```

```
```

Finally, we can use these decorator classes to add new behavior to our coffee types at runtime.

```
Coffee simpleLatte = new Latte();
System.out.println("Simple Latte: " + simpleLatte.getPrice() +
", " + simpleLatte.getIngredients());
Coffee latteWithWhippedCream = new WhippedCreamDecorator(new
Latte());
System.out.println("Latte with Whipped Cream: " +
latteWithWhippedCream.getPrice() + ", " +
latteWithWhippedCream.getIngredients());
Coffee cappuccinoWithCaramelSyrup = new
CaramelSyrupDecorator(new Cappuccino());
System.out.println("Cappuccino with Caramel Syrup: " +
cappuccinoWithCaramelSyrup.getPrice() + ", " +
cappuccinoWithCaramelSyrup.getIngredients());
``
```

` Output: `
```
``
```

```
Simple Latte: 4.50, Espresso, steamed milk, and foam Latte
with Whipped Cream: 6.00, Espresso, steamed milk, foam, and
whipped cream Cappuccino with Caramel Syrup: 7.00, Espresso,
steamed milk, foam, and caramel syrup
```

```
```

As we can see, by using the decorator pattern, we were able to add new functionality to our coffee types without modifying their original classes. This makes our code more flexible and scalable, adhering to the principle of open-closed design.

Conclusion

In this chapter, we have learned about the decorator pattern, its benefits, and how it can be implemented in a codebase using a simple coffee shop example. The decorator pattern is a powerful technique that allows for the dynamic addition of new behavior to an object at runtime, making code more flexible and maintainable. By using this pattern, developers can adhere to good design principles, such as code reuse and separation of concerns.

Chapter 15: The Power of the Decorator Pattern

Definition

The decorator pattern is a design pattern that allows us to dynamically add new behavior to an object without changing its existing code. It is one of the many structural patterns in software engineering that allows us to compose functionality rather than inherit it. This means that with the decorator pattern, we can add or remove features to an object at runtime, making it a powerful tool for extending the functionality of our software.

Advantages

One of the main advantages of the decorator pattern is that it follows the open-closed principle, which states that software entities should be open for extension but closed for modification. This allows us to add new features to an object without altering its existing code, making it more maintainable and scalable. Additionally, the decorator pattern allows us to create a flexible and modular design, making it easier to add or remove functionality as needed.Another advantage of the decorator pattern is that it allows for the creation of a wide range of variations for an object. By using multiple decorators, we can combine different behaviors and features to create unique combinations, providing greater flexibility and customization in our software. This not only makes our code more efficient but also leads to a more user-friendly experience for our clients.

Implementation

To understand the implementation of the decorator pattern, let's consider an example of a car manufacturing company. The company produces various models of cars, each with different features and pricing. However, they want to offer customization options to their clients, such as adding extra features like a navigation system, sunroof, or leather seats. Instead of creating a separate class for each customization option, they can use the decorator pattern to add these features dynamically. First, we would have our base class, the Car, which would have common properties and methods for all the models. Then, we would have concrete car classes such as Sedan, SUV, and Hatchback, which would inherit from the Car class and add specific features like engine type, number of seats, and price. Next, we would create a decorator class, let's call it CarDecorator, which would also inherit from the Car class. This decorator class would have a reference to the Car object and add additional features by extending its behavior without changing its core functionality. To add a customization option, such as a sunroof, we would create a SunroofDecorator class, which would inherit from the CarDecorator class and add the sunroof feature. We could continue adding decorators for other options, such as NavigationDecorator and LeatherSeatsDecorator, and then combine them to create various combinations like a SunroofSUV with Navigation and Leather Seats.The client could then choose the desired combination of features, and the decorator pattern would dynamically add them to the base car object at runtime. This not only ensures that the base car class remains unchanged but also allows for easy addition or removal of options without affecting the rest of the code.

Conclusion

The decorator pattern is a powerful tool in software design, offering many advantages such as scalability, modular design, and flexibility. Its implementation allows for dynamic addition of features, making it a popular choice among developers. By using this pattern, we can create efficient, maintainable, and customizable software that meets the diverse needs of our clients. So next time you are faced with a situation where you need to add functionality to an existing object, remember the decorator pattern and its many benefits.

Chapter 16: Mediator Pattern

This often overlooked Design Pattern is a powerful tool in a Software Engineer's toolkit. It is a behavioral pattern that helps to promote loose coupling among multiple objects in a system. In this chapter, we will explore the concept of Mediator Pattern, its real-world applications, and the benefits it brings to software engineering.

Explanation

The Mediator Pattern, also known as the Publish-Subscribe Pattern, is a design pattern that promotes loose coupling and communication between multiple objects within a system. It acts as a mediator, or a middleman, between these objects, helping them communicate with each other without having to directly reference each other. This pattern follows the principle of "one-to-many" communication, where a single object (the Mediator) handles the interaction between multiple objects instead of each object directly communicating with one another.In simpler terms, the Mediator Pattern allows objects in a system to work together without needing to know about each other, reducing dependencies and making the system more flexible and easier to maintain. It also centralizes the communication logic, making it easier to add, remove, or modify the behavior of the system.

Real-world Examples

One of the most well-known examples of the Mediator Pattern is the air traffic control system in airports. In this scenario, the control tower acts as the mediator between different aircraft, guiding them in and out of the airport safely and efficiently. Without the control tower, the aircraft would have to communicate with each other directly, resulting in chaos and potential accidents. In software development, the Mediator Pattern can be seen in user interface components, where there is a need for interaction between various elements without them directly referencing each other. For example, in a chat application, the mediator handles the communication between users without involving direct communication between individual users.Another real-world example of the Mediator Pattern is a stock exchange system, where the stockbrokers communicate with each other through a centralized mediator instead of contacting each other directly. This helps to reduce dependencies and allows for better scalability and flexibility in the system.

Benefits

The Mediator Pattern brings several benefits to software engineering. Some of these benefits include decreased dependencies, increased modularity, better maintainability, and scalability. By reducing the dependencies between objects, the Mediator Pattern promotes flexibility and makes it easier to modify the behavior of the system. It also allows for better code reuse, as new objects can be added to the system without affecting the existing ones. Moreover, the Mediator Pattern improves modularity by centralizing the communication logic in a single object. This makes it easier to manage and maintain, and also improves the readability of the codebase. The pattern also boosts the scalability of the system by enabling new objects to be added and removed without affecting the existing ones. This is especially useful in systems that require frequent updates and modifications.In addition to these benefits, the Mediator Pattern also promotes a more organized and structured approach to software development, resulting in better communication and collaboration among team members.

Conclusion

The Mediator Pattern is a key design pattern that every Software Engineer should be familiar with. It allows for better communication and collaboration between objects in a system, resulting in a more flexible, maintainable, and scalable codebase. With real-world applications in various industries, the Mediator Pattern is a valuable tool that can greatly improve the quality of software engineering.

Chapter 17: Observer Pattern

Definition

The Observer Pattern is a design pattern that allows for communication between objects in a loosely coupled manner. It is a behavioral pattern that promotes the highly sought-after qualities of flexibility and maintainability in software systems. This pattern is commonly used in applications where multiple components or objects require frequent updates when changes are made to a particular subject or data.

Advantages

One of the main advantages of the Observer Pattern is its ability to decouple objects and promote a more streamlined design. Rather than tightly coupling objects together, the Observer Pattern allows for a more flexible and modular structure. This allows for easy maintenance and updates without having to make changes to multiple components of the system. The Observer Pattern also promotes reusability and extensibility in software. By separating the subject and observer objects, it becomes easier to add new observers without making any changes to the existing code. This way, new features can be easily added without affecting the overall functionality of the system.Furthermore, the Observer Pattern promotes a high level of synchronization among objects. Whenever a change is made to the subject, it automatically notifies all the observers, ensuring that they are always updated with the latest information. This feature can be particularly useful in situations where real-time data updates are required.

Implementation

Implementing the Observer Pattern involves creating two main components – a subject and an observer. The subject is the object that is being observed, while the observer is the object that is notified whenever a change is made to the subject. To implement this pattern, the subject must maintain a list of observers and provide methods for adding or removing observers from this list. Whenever a change is made to the subject, it is responsible for notifying all the observers in the list by invoking an update method. On the other hand, observers must implement an update method that specifies how they handle changes made to the subject. This method can be customized for each observer, allowing for different reactions to the same change in the subject. It is also important to note that the Observer Pattern can be implemented using either a push or pull approach. In the push approach, the subject sends the necessary information to the observers, while in the pull approach, the observers retrieve the information from the subject when needed.

In conclusion, the Observer Pattern is a powerful and flexible tool that can greatly enhance the design and development of software systems. Its advantages of decoupling, extensibility and synchronization make it a valuable pattern to have in one's arsenal. By understanding its definition and how to implement it, software engineers can effectively utilize the Observer Pattern to create robust and maintainable software.

Chapter 18: Observer Pattern

Explanation

The Observer pattern is a behavioral design pattern that allows an object, known as the subject, to maintain a list of its dependents, known as observers, and notify them automatically of any changes in its state. This pattern promotes loose coupling between the subject and its observers, providing a more flexible and maintainable code design. The subject and observers are able to communicate without being tightly coupled, as they only need to know each other's interfaces and not their concrete implementations.

Use Cases

The Observer pattern is commonly used in many software systems and applications, such as:

- Chat applications, where users can subscribe to a channel and receive notifications whenever a new message is sent

- Stock market systems, where investors can subscribe to stock prices and receive updates in real-time

- Social media platforms, where users can follow other users and get notified of their posts and updatesThis pattern can also be used in situations where there is a one-to-many relationship between objects, and the changes in one object's state need to be reflected in the others.

Pros and Cons

Pros:

- Loose coupling: As mentioned earlier, the Observer pattern promotes loose coupling between the subject and its observers, making it easier to maintain and modify the code.

- Flexibility: This pattern allows for dynamically adding and removing observers from the subject without affecting its functionality.

- Scalability: The Observer pattern is scalable, meaning that it can handle an infinite number of observers without impacting the subject's performance.

- Easy to implement: The basic structure of the Observer pattern is easy to understand and implement, making it a good choice for novice developers.

Cons:

- Unexpected updates: If not implemented carefully, changes in the subject's state can lead to unexpected updates in the observers, sometimes resulting in performance issues or even bugs.

- Order dependency: The order in which observers are notified of changes can have a significant impact on the overall functionality of the system. This can lead to the need for careful planning and testing to ensure the desired outcome.

- Memory leaks: Improper implementation of the Observer pattern can lead to memory leaks, as observers may not be properly removed and can continue to listen for changes even when no longer needed.

Conclusion

The Observer pattern is an essential tool in the software engineer's toolkit, allowing for flexible and maintainable code design. Its benefits, such as loose coupling and scalability, outweigh its potential drawbacks, making it a popular choice in various applications. As with any design pattern, it is crucial to carefully consider its implementation and potential impact on the overall system. With its ability to handle one-to-many relationships and automatic notifications, the Observer pattern can greatly enhance the functionality and usability of software systems.

Chapter 19: Strategy Pattern - The Versatile Solution for Dynamic Behavior

Definition

The Strategy Pattern is a behavioral design pattern that allows for the dynamic selection of an algorithm at runtime. It encapsulates an interchangeable behavior within a class, allowing it to switch between various strategies without affecting the client.In simpler terms, the Strategy Pattern allows for flexible behavior by separating it from the main class and delegating it to a group of interchangeable classes. This allows for a more customizable and extensible codebase for dynamic behavior.

Implementation

To understand the Strategy Pattern better, let us consider a real-world example. Imagine you are running a delivery service and you have different modes of delivery, such as by car, bike, or airplane. Each mode of delivery has its own set of behaviors and calculations, but the ultimate goal is the same - to deliver the package to its destination. Traditionally, you would create different delivery classes for each mode, but this can become cumbersome as more modes are added in the future. The Strategy Pattern offers a more elegant solution by creating a Delivery Strategy interface that each mode implements. This interface defines the behavior for delivering the package, such as calculating the time and cost.The main delivery class then has a reference to the Delivery Strategy, which can be set to any mode at runtime. This way, the main class doesn't need to know the specifics of each mode and remains decoupled from the delivery behavior. This allows for easy addition of new modes without having to modify the main class.

Advantages

The Strategy Pattern offers many advantages, making it a popular choice among software engineers. Some of the key advantages are:

1. Flexible and Extensible:

By separating the behavior into interchangeable classes, the Strategy Pattern offers a flexible and extensible codebase. New strategies can be added without changing the main class, making it easy to adapt to changing requirements.

2. Easy to Maintain:

The Strategy Pattern promotes code reuse and follows the open-closed principle, making it easier to maintain the codebase. Changes in one strategy do not affect the others, leading to a more stable and maintainable codebase.

3. Improved Readability and Maintainability:

With the use of meaningful strategy names, the code becomes more readable and easier to maintain. This promotes a clean and organized codebase, making it easier to understand and modify in the future.

4. Facilitates Testing:

By isolating the behavior into separate classes, the Strategy Pattern makes it easier to test each strategy individually. This promotes efficient debugging and helps in ensuring the overall quality of the codebase.

5. Encourages Separation of Concerns:

The Strategy Pattern follows the single responsibility principle by separating the behavior from the main class. This encourages separation of concerns and promotes a more modular codebase.

6. Promotes Reusability:

As behaviors are encapsulated into their own classes, they can be reused in other parts of the codebase. This promotes the reuse of code and reduces the need for duplicating code for similar functionality.

7. Adheres to Design Principles:

The Strategy Pattern follows the SOLID principles of object-oriented design, making it a reliable and effective solution for dynamic behavior. It also promotes code that is more maintainable, extensible, and reusable.

In conclusion, the Strategy Pattern is a powerful and versatile solution for managing dynamic behavior in software applications. It offers many benefits such as maintainability, testability, and extensibility, making it a popular choice among software engineers. So the next time you need to implement dynamic behavior in your code, consider using the Strategy Pattern for a more elegant and efficient solution.

Chapter 20: State Pattern

Explanation

The State Pattern is a behavioral design pattern that allows an object to change its behavior based on its internal state. This means that the object can have different behaviors depending on its current state, making its behavior more dynamic and flexible.In simpler terms, the State Pattern allows an object to act differently depending on the state it is currently in. This eliminates the need for conditional statements and makes the code more organized and maintainable.

Pros and Cons

Pros

- Makes code more organized and maintainable by eliminating the need for conditional statements

- Allows objects to change their behavior at runtime

- Encourages the use of small, reusable objects

- Offers a cleaner and more flexible solution compared to a switch-case statement approach

- Facilitates the addition of new states without affecting the existing code

- Helps in implementing the Open-Closed principle by allowing code to be extended without modification

Cons

- Can sometimes create an unnecessary number of classes if not implemented properly

- Can be complex to understand for beginners

- Might not be suitable for small, simple applications

Real-world Examples

One real-world example of the State Pattern is a vending machine. The vending machine has different behaviors based on its current state (e.g. ready to dispense, out of stock, out of change). By using the State Pattern, the vending machine can change its behavior without the need for conditional statements, making the code more organized and easier to maintain. Another example is a media player app. The media player has different behaviors depending on its current state (e.g. playing, paused, stopped). By using the State Pattern, the media player can change its behavior dynamically, offering a more flexible and clean solution compared to a switch-case statement approach.In the world of gaming, the State Pattern is also widely used. Games often have different states (e.g. main menu, paused, game over) that require different behaviors from the game's objects. By using the State Pattern, developers can easily add new states without having to modify the existing code, making the code more maintainable.

The State Pattern is a useful tool for making code more organized and maintainable by allowing objects to change their behavior dynamically depending on their current state. It offers a cleaner and more flexible solution compared to a switch-case statement approach and promotes the use of small, reusable objects. However, it may not be suitable for simple applications and can sometimes create an unnecessary number of classes if not implemented properly. With its real-world examples, we can see how the State Pattern has been used to improve the functionality and flexibility of various systems.

Chapter 21: Template Method Pattern

Definition

The Template Method Pattern is a behavioral design pattern that is used to define the skeleton or structure of an algorithm and allows subclasses to redefine certain steps without changing the overall structure of the algorithm. In simpler terms, it follows the "don't call us, we'll call you" principle, where the overall process is defined by the superclass, but specific steps can be left to be defined by subclasses.

Implementation

To implement the Template Method Pattern, there are two key components: an abstract superclass that defines the overall algorithm and concrete subclasses that implement the specific steps.Let's take a simple example of making a cup of tea using the Template Method Pattern. Our abstract superclass, "HotBeverage," will define the overall process of making a hot beverage. It will have a method called "makeHotBeverage" that will call other methods. These methods, such as "boilWater," "addTeaBag," and "pourHotWater," are left abstract, to be implemented by the subclasses according to their specific requirements. In our example, we will have two concrete subclasses, "Tea" and "Coffee," that will implement these abstract methods.

Use Cases

The Template Method Pattern is commonly used in situations where there is a need for a common algorithm with slight variations in implementation. Here are a few use cases where the Template Method Pattern is applicable:

1. Making hot beverages (as demonstrated in our example).

2. Online shopping, where the overall process is the same but the payment method may differ.

3. Creating different types of reports that follow a similar structure but have different data sources.

4. Building a game with different levels, where the overall gameplay is the same but the difficulty level may vary.

5. Setting up a framework for web development, where the overall structure is predefined, but the specific components and its implementations may differ.In all these cases, the Template Method Pattern provides a flexible and reusable solution by separating the overall process from its individual steps, allowing variations to be easily incorporated without impacting the core algorithm.

The Template Method Pattern is a powerful tool in a programmer's arsenal that allows for easy code reuse and extensibility. By separating the overall process from its individual steps, it provides a flexible and robust solution to handle situations where the overall structure remains the same, but specific steps may differ. So, the next time you find yourself in a situation that requires a common algorithm with slight variations, think of the Template Method Pattern and let it guide you towards an elegant and efficient solution.

Chapter 22: The Bridge Pattern

The bridge pattern is a structural design pattern that allows for decoupling between an abstraction and its implementation. This chapter will explore the benefits, drawbacks, and real-world examples of using the bridge pattern in software engineering.

Explanation

The bridge pattern is used when there is a need to separate an abstraction from its implementation, allowing them to vary independently. This is achieved by having an abstraction class that contains a reference to an interface, called the implementation. The abstraction can then delegate specific tasks to the implementation, without worrying about the details of how it is implemented.The primary goal of the bridge pattern is to promote loose coupling between classes, which leads to improved flexibility and maintainability of the code. This is because changes made to the implementation class will not affect the abstraction class, and vice versa. Additionally, the bridge pattern allows for a single implementation to be used by multiple abstractions, reducing code duplication.

Example Usage

A classic example of using the bridge pattern is in designing UI elements for a mobile application. These UI elements, such as buttons and text fields, may have different implementations for different platforms (e.g., iOS and Android). To ensure the UI elements have a consistent appearance and behavior, the bridge pattern can be used.The abstraction class in this scenario would be the UI element, and the implementation would be the platform-specific code. By using the bridge pattern, changes made to the implementation for one platform will not affect the other platforms. This allows for easy maintenance and updating of the codebase.

Pros and Cons

There are several advantages to using the bridge pattern in software engineering. First and foremost, it promotes loose coupling between classes, which leads to increased flexibility and maintainability of the code. It also allows for a single implementation to be used by multiple abstractions, reducing code duplication. Additionally, the bridge pattern can be used to support new platforms, without having to make changes to the existing codebase. However, there are also some drawbacks to consider when using the bridge pattern. One potential issue is the increased complexity of the code. With the abstraction and implementation classes communicating through a bridge, it can become challenging to understand the flow of the code. This can make debugging and troubleshooting more complicated.Furthermore, the bridge pattern may not be suitable for all scenarios. It is most effective when there is a clear separation between the abstraction and the implementation. If this is not the case, implementing the bridge pattern may not provide any significant benefits and could potentially complicate the design.

Real-World Examples

Aside from UI elements in mobile applications, there are several other real-world examples of using the bridge pattern. One common use case is in database systems. In this scenario, the abstraction class would represent the high-level database operations, such as querying and updating data, while the implementation class would handle the specific database engine being used. Another popular example is in video game development. With different platforms, such as consoles and PCs, the bridge pattern can be used to handle the various input devices and display capabilities. This allows the game to be ported to different platforms with ease, without having to make significant changes to the codebase.

In conclusion, the bridge pattern is a powerful design pattern that promotes loose coupling between classes and allows for independent variation of abstraction and implementation. By understanding its benefits, drawbacks, and real-world examples, software engineers can effectively use the bridge pattern in their projects to improve code maintainability and flexibility.

Chapter 23: Bridge Pattern

The beauty of software engineering lies in its ability to solve complex problems and simplify everyday tasks. Design patterns are the backbone of this process, providing proven solutions to recurring design problems. One such pattern is the Bridge Pattern, which aims to decouple an abstraction from its implementation. In this chapter, we will delve into the world of Bridge Pattern and explore its definition, real-world examples, and benefits.

Definition

The Bridge Pattern falls under the category of structural design patterns. It is used to separate an abstraction from its implementation, allowing them to vary independently. This means that the abstraction and implementation can be modified without affecting each other, ultimately leading to a flexible and extensible system.At its core, the Bridge Pattern uses the concept of encapsulation to remove dependencies between classes. It creates a bridge between an abstraction and its implementation, allowing them to interact without the need for a tight coupling. This promotes code reuse and makes the system more maintainable.

Real-world Examples

To understand the Bridge Pattern better, let's look at some real-world examples where it has been used.

1. User Interface Design
In user interface design, the Bridge Pattern is often used to separate the graphical interface from its underlying platform. This allows the user interface to be tailored to different operating systems or devices, without having to modify the core code.For example, the work of creating icons for an application can be delegated to a separate class, which is then connected to the main program through a bridge. This not only simplifies the code but also ensures a consistent user experience across different platforms.

2. Database Connectivity

Another common example of the Bridge Pattern can be seen in database connectivity. It is used to decouple the database implementation from the application layer, allowing different types of databases to be connected without changing the code.For instance, if a business decides to switch from a relational database to a NoSQL database, they can simply create a new bridge class for the NoSQL database and plug it into the existing system without having to make any major changes.

Benefits

Now that we have seen some examples of the Bridge Pattern in action, let's discuss its benefits.

1. Promotes Code Reuse

As mentioned earlier, the Bridge Pattern promotes code reuse by separating an abstraction from its implementation. This means that the same abstraction can be used with different implementations, saving time and effort in the development process.

2. Enhances Flexibility

By decoupling the abstraction and implementation, the Bridge Pattern makes the system more flexible. This allows for easier modifications and updates without affecting the entire codebase. New implementations can also be added without disrupting the existing code, making the system more adaptable to changes.

3. Improves Maintainability

Tightly coupled code can be a nightmare for developers when it comes to maintenance. The Bridge Pattern resolves this issue by isolating the abstraction and implementation, making it easier to maintain and debug the codebase.

4. Facilitates Extensibility

In a constantly evolving technological landscape, it is crucial to have a system that can easily adapt to new requirements. The Bridge Pattern allows for seamless integration of new implementations, making the system more extensible and future-proof.

5. Encourages Separation of Concerns

The Bridge Pattern encourages a clear separation of concerns, as it separates the abstraction from the implementation. This makes the code more organized and easier to understand, reducing the chances of errors and bugs.

In Conclusion

The Bridge Pattern is a powerful design pattern that promotes code reuse, flexibility, maintainability, and extensibility. It allows for a clear separation of concerns and makes the codebase more organized and manageable. By using this pattern, software engineers can create robust and adaptable systems that can stand the test of time.

Chapter 24: Prototype vs. Cloneable

Comparison

In the world of software engineering, there are often multiple ways to accomplish a task or solve a problem. This is also true when it comes to creating new objects. Two common approaches in this area are the use of the Prototype pattern and the Cloneable interface. While both can be used for creating and copying objects, they have distinct differences that set them apart. Let's take a closer look at the comparison between Prototype and Cloneable.

Examples

The Prototype pattern involves creating a prototype or template object that serves as a blueprint for creating new objects. This prototype object is copied and any changes made to it will be reflected in all of its copies. An example of this can be seen in the creation of a new user account in an app. The prototype object would contain all the basic information and settings for a user, and by using the Prototype pattern, new user accounts can be easily created by copying and altering the prototype.On the other hand, the Cloneable interface is used for making an exact copy of an existing object. This allows for the creation of multiple identical objects with the same properties and values. An example of this can be seen in a shopping app where a user wants to purchase multiple quantities of the same product. By using the Cloneable interface, the app can quickly and easily create identical copies of the product object, saving time and effort in manually creating each one.

Best Practices

So, which approach is the best one to use? The answer is not that simple as it depends on the specific context and requirements of the project. However, here are some best practices that can help guide your decision:

- Use the Prototype pattern when the creation of objects depends on the context or settings of an existing object.

- Use the Cloneable interface when there is a need for multiple copies of the same object with the same properties.

- Consider using both approaches together if the project calls for it. For example, the Prototype pattern can be used to create prototype objects, and then the Cloneable interface can be used to make copies of these prototypes.

- Take into account the performance and memory implications of each approach. The Prototype pattern can be more efficient when only a few objects need to be created, while the Cloneable interface can quickly become a memory hog when creating large numbers of copies.

In the end, the choice between Prototype and Cloneable will depend on the specific needs and goals of your project. Whichever approach you choose, it's important to have a clear understanding of their differences and best practices so that you can utilize them effectively.In this chapter, we've explored the comparison between Prototype and Cloneable, as well as provided some examples and best practices for their use. By understanding these two different approaches, you can make informed decisions when creating and copying objects in your software engineering projects. Happy coding!

Chapter 25: Adapter vs. Decorator

Differences

When it comes to designing software applications, developers often face the challenge of designing a system that is both flexible and maintainable. Two design patterns that can help achieve these goals are the adapter and decorator patterns. While they may seem similar in some aspects, they have distinct differences that make them both unique and suitable for different scenarios. The adapter pattern is a structural design pattern that allows two incompatible interfaces to work together. It acts as a bridge between the client and the target, translating requests from the client into a format that the target can understand. On the other hand, the decorator pattern is a behavioral design pattern that adds functionality to an existing object dynamically, without altering its original structure. It acts as a wrapper around the target object, providing additional or modified behavior.The main difference between the two patterns lies in their intent. The adapter pattern primarily focuses on interoperability between two systems, while the decorator pattern focuses on enhancing the behavior of a single object. Both patterns achieve these goals in different ways, making them powerful tools in a software engineer's toolkit.

Real-world Examples

Let's delve deeper into the differences between these two patterns by examining some real-world examples. Consider a scenario where a computer science professor wants to build an application that can convert existing C++ code into Java. Since the two languages have different syntax and conventions, the professor decides to use the adapter pattern to bridge the gap between the two languages. Using the adapter pattern, the professor can create an adapter class that translates the C++ code into Java code. The adapter class acts as the bridge between the C++ code and the Java code, allowing the professor to seamlessly convert the code from one language to another. In this example, the adapter pattern is used to achieve interoperability between two systems that otherwise have different structures and conventions.On the other hand, consider a scenario where a fashion designer wants to add embellishments to a dress. The designer could use the decorator pattern to add different decorations, such as lace, beads, or embroidery to the dress. The decorator pattern is a perfect fit for this scenario, as it allows the designer to add additional behavior to the dress without altering its original structure. The designer can also combine multiple decorators to create unique and intricate designs, showcasing the pattern's dynamic nature.

When to Use

Now that we have a clear understanding of the differences between the adapter and decorator patterns let's explore when to use each one. Use the adapter pattern when you want to make two incompatible interfaces work together seamlessly. This pattern is helpful when dealing with legacy code or third-party libraries that have different conventions and structures. The adapter pattern also promotes code reuse, as it allows the existing code to work with new systems without the need for significant modifications. On the other hand, use the decorator pattern when you want to add behavior to an object dynamically, without changing its original structure. This pattern is useful when you have a specific base behavior that needs to be enhanced or modified based on specific conditions. The decorator pattern also promotes flexibility and extensibility, as decorators can be added or removed at runtime, providing a wide range of possible combinations.

In conclusion, the adapter and decorator patterns may seem similar at first glance, but their differences set them apart in terms of intent and application. As a software engineer, it is essential to understand the strengths and weaknesses of each pattern to make informed design decisions. With the power of these two patterns at their disposal, developers can build flexible, maintainable, and robust software systems.

Chapter 26: Abstract Class vs. Interface

Software engineers are often faced with the decision between using an abstract class or an interface when designing their applications. Both of these are important concepts in object-oriented programming and have their own unique strengths and uses. In this chapter, we will explore the comparison between abstract classes and interfaces, their advantages, and best practices for using them effectively in software design.

Comparison

Before·diving into the comparison, let's first define what an abstract class and an interface are. An abstract class is a class that cannot be instantiated and is intended to be inherited by other classes. It contains abstract methods, which are declared but not implemented, and concrete methods, which have an implemented body. An interface, on the other hand, is a blueprint of methods that must be implemented by a class that implements it. An interface can only have abstract methods and constants, without any implemented methods.One of the main differences between an abstract class and an interface is that a class can only extend one abstract class but can implement multiple interfaces. In terms of usage, an abstract class is suitable for a class hierarchy, where the abstract class defines common methods and the subclasses implement specific behaviors. An interface, on the other hand, is useful for defining a set of behaviors that a class must implement, without providing any implementation details.

Advantages

Now let's shift our focus to the advantages of using an abstract class or an interface in software design.

Abstract Class Advantages:
1. Code Reusability: Abstract classes can be extended by multiple subclasses, allowing for code reuse. This means that the same functionality can be implemented in different subclasses without duplicating code.

2. Partial Implementation: Abstract classes can have both abstract and concrete

methods, allowing certain functionalities to be implemented in the abstract class itself. This can be useful for defining common behaviors that all subclasses must have.

3. Flexibility: An abstract class can be extended and modified at any time, allowing for flexibility in design.

Interface Advantages:
1. Multiple Implementations: As mentioned earlier, a class can implement multiple interfaces, allowing for more flexibility in terms of functionality.

2. Loose Coupling: Interfaces promote loose coupling between classes, as the implementation details are not tied to the interface itself. This allows for easier maintenance and changes in the future.

3. Polymorphism: Implementing an interface allows for polymorphism, where an object can take on different forms depending on the interface it implements. This can be useful for creating generic methods and classes.

Best Practices

Now that we have explored the comparison and advantages of abstract classes and interfaces, let's discuss some best practices for using them in software design.

1. Use abstract classes when defining a class hierarchy: If you have a set of related classes that share common methods and behaviors, an abstract class is a better choice. It allows for code reuse and promotes a more organized and structured class hierarchy.

2. Use interfaces when defining a set of behaviors: Interfaces are useful for defining a set of behaviors that a class must implement. This allows for more flexibility in terms of functionality and promotes loose coupling.

3. Avoid using abstract classes and interfaces unnecessarily: It is important to not overuse abstract classes and interfaces in your design. Too many abstract classes can lead to a complicated and confusing hierarchy, while too many interfaces can cause unnecessary coupling between classes.

4. Consider future changes and maintenance: When designing with abstract classes

and interfaces, it is important to consider potential future changes and maintenance. This can help determine which approach would be more suitable and efficient for the long term.

In conclusion, abstract classes and interfaces are both important concepts in software engineering, with their own unique strengths and uses. In order to make the best design decision, it is important to understand their comparison, advantages, and best practices. By following these best practices, you can create more efficient, flexible, and maintainable software systems using these powerful object-oriented programming concepts.

Chapter 27: Inversion of Control and Dependency Injection

Explanation

Software engineers are often faced with the challenge of designing and building complex systems that are both efficient and maintainable. One of the key principles that can help achieve these goals is the concept of inversion of control (IoC). This is a design pattern in which the flow of control is inverted from traditional programming models, allowing for more flexibility, extensibility, and testability in software development.At its core, the idea of inversion of control is about separating the construction of objects from their dependencies. In traditional programming models, objects create their own dependencies, meaning they are tightly coupled and difficult to change or test in isolation. In contrast, with inversion of control, dependencies are provided to an object rather than created by the object itself. This is where dependency injection comes into play.

Dependency Injection

Dependency injection is a technique used to implement inversion of control in software design. It involves providing objects with their dependencies from an external source, rather than having the objects create their own dependencies. This not only decouples objects from their dependencies, but also allows for easier testing, maintenance, and scalability of the codebase. In a typical dependency injection scenario, there are three main components: the client, the injector, and the services. The client is the code that requires a specific service to perform its tasks, the injector is responsible for providing the client with the necessary services, and the services are the objects that are injected into the client.There are several approaches to implementing dependency injection, such as constructor injection, setter injection, and interface injection. In constructor injection, the dependencies are provided through the constructor of the client class. In setter injection, the dependencies are provided through setter methods. And in interface injection, the client implements an interface that defines the necessary dependencies.

Example Implementation

To better understand dependency injection, let's look at a simple example of a dependency injection framework. We will use the popular Java framework, Spring, as an example. Let's say we have a client class, called PaymentService, that needs to process payments for an e-commerce website. In order to process payments, we need a PaymentGateway service. Traditionally, we may have something like this:

```
public class PaymentService {
    private PaymentGateway paymentGateway;
    public PaymentService() {
        this.paymentGateway = new PaymentGateway();
    } //...other methods and logic }
```

This is how a traditional non-inverted control approach might look. The PaymentService class creates its own dependency, PaymentGateway, using the new operator. This creates tight coupling between the two classes and makes it difficult to change or test them in isolation.To implement dependency injection, we can use the Spring framework and its dependency injection capabilities. First, we need to define the PaymentGateway as a bean in our Spring configuration file. This tells the Spring container how to create the PaymentGateway object when it is needed. For example:

Next, we need to modify our PaymentService class to use dependency injection instead of creating its own instance of PaymentGateway. We can do this by using the @Autowired annotation to specify that the dependency should be injected by Spring. For example:

```
public class PaymentService {
    @Autowired private PaymentGateway paymentGateway;
    public PaymentService() { //no longer needed since
dependency is injected } //...other methods and logic}
```

In this example, Spring will automatically inject the PaymentGateway object into the

PaymentService class whenever it is needed, without the need for us to create it ourselves.By implementing dependency injection, we have decoupled our objects and made them more flexible and manageable. We can easily switch out the implementation of the PaymentGateway, or add new dependencies to the PaymentService, without having to modify the code. This results in cleaner, more maintainable code that is easier to test and extend.

Closing Thoughts

Inversion of control and dependency injection may seem like a small concept, but they can have a big impact on the design and scalability of software systems. By separating the creation of objects from their dependencies, we can achieve more efficient, maintainable, and testable code. And with the help of dependency injection frameworks such as Spring, implementing this design pattern has become easier and more widely adopted in the software engineering world.So next time you're faced with a complex software design problem, remember the principles of inversion of control and dependency injection, and see how they can help you create more efficient and maintainable solutions.

Chapter 28: Dependency Injection Frameworks

Explanation:

Software engineering is a constantly evolving field, always seeking out ways to improve efficiency, reduce errors, and increase overall quality of the end product. One of the ways this is achieved is through the use of dependency injection frameworks. These frameworks provide a way to manage dependencies between different modules or components in a software system. In this chapter, we will dive into the details of dependency injection frameworks, their types, and the pros and cons of using them.

Types:

There are three main types of dependency injection frameworks: Constructor Injection, Setter Injection, and Interface Injection. Constructor Injection is the most common type of dependency injection and involves injecting dependencies through a class constructor. This means that the dependencies are declared as private fields in the class and are passed in through the constructor during instantiation. This ensures that the class has all the necessary dependencies before it can be used. Setter Injection, on the other hand, involves injecting dependencies through setter methods. This allows for more flexibility as the dependencies can be changed or updated at runtime. However, it can also lead to potential errors if the dependencies are not set correctly.Interface Injection is a less common type of dependency injection and involves injecting dependencies by implementing an interface. This allows for even more flexibility as the dependencies can be changed by implementing different interfaces. However, it also requires more upfront planning and can make the code more complex.

Pros and Cons:

Like any tool or framework, dependency injection frameworks have their own set of pros and cons that should be considered when deciding whether to use them in a project.

Pros:

1. Improved Testability

One of the main benefits of using dependency injection frameworks is improved testability. By removing direct dependencies between classes, it becomes easier to isolate and test individual components. This allows for more efficient testing and can reduce the time and effort required for testing.

2. Easier Maintenance

Another advantage of using dependency injection frameworks is that it makes maintenance and updates easier. As dependencies are declared and managed separately, making changes to one component will not affect other components. This allows for more flexibility and reduces the risk of unintended consequences.

3. Encourages Modularity

Dependency injection frameworks promote modularity by breaking down a complex system into smaller, more manageable components. This not only makes the code more organized and easier to maintain, but it also allows for easier scalability in the future.

Cons:

1. Steep Learning Curve

One of the drawbacks of using dependency injection frameworks is that they can have a steep learning curve. Understanding the concepts and implementing them correctly can be challenging for those new to the framework. This can result in mistakes and potential errors in the code.

2. More Complex Code

As dependency injection frameworks involve more layers and components, the code can become more complex and harder to understand. This can make it more difficult for new developers to jump into the project and can also lead to performance issues if not implemented properly.

3. Overuse Can Lead to Problems

While dependency injection frameworks can be beneficial when used correctly, overusing them can lead to problems. It is important to strike a balance and only use them when necessary. Otherwise, it can lead to bloated code and decrease the overall performance of the system.

In conclusion, dependency injection frameworks offer many advantages for managing dependencies in a software system. They improve testability, ease maintenance, and promote modularity. However, they also have some drawbacks such as a steep learning curve, more complex code, and the potential for problems if overused. As with any technology, it is important to carefully consider the needs of the project before implementing a dependency injection framework. With proper planning and implementation, these frameworks can greatly enhance the efficiency and quality of a software system.

Chapter 29: Inversion of Control

Definition

Inversion of Control (IoC) is an architectural pattern in software engineering that refers to the framework or container controlling the flow of program execution. In simpler terms, it simply means that instead of the application controlling the flow of execution, the framework or container manages the dependencies and control flow.

Advantages

One of the biggest advantages of using IoC is better maintainability and flexibility of the code. With the framework controlling the dependencies, the code becomes more loosely coupled and easier to modify or update. This also results in easier unit testing and debugging as the code can now be broken down into smaller components.Another advantage of IoC is its ability to promote modular and reusable code. Since the dependencies are managed by the framework, the different modules can be easily integrated and used in different parts of the application. This also leads to a more organized and structured code base, making it easier for developers to collaborate and work on different parts of the project.

Implementation

IoC can be implemented in various ways, with the two most common methods being Dependency Injection (DI) and Service Locator. In DI, the framework is responsible for injecting the required dependencies into a class or component, while with Service Locator, the framework acts as a central repository for all the dependencies and can be called upon to retrieve them when needed. There are also different types of DI, including Constructor Injection, Setter Injection, and Interface Injection. Constructor Injection involves passing the dependencies as parameters in the constructor of a class. Setter Injection, as the name suggests, uses setter methods to inject the dependencies. Interface Injection, on the other hand, uses interfaces to define the required dependencies and their implementation, allowing for more flexibility in changing the dependencies at runtime. To implement IoC, first, we need to choose a suitable IoC container, such as Spring, Autofac, or Unity. These containers come with their own methods of managing dependencies and provide various features such as lifecycle management, dependency resolution, and integration with other frameworks. Next, we need to identify the dependencies of each class and define them in the container. This can be done using annotations, XML configuration, or through code. Once the dependencies are defined, the framework will take care of injecting them when the class is instantiated.Overall, the implementation of IoC depends on the specific framework and the needs of the application. However, the basic principles remain the same, with the framework managing the control flow and dependencies, and the code becoming more modular and maintainable.

Closing thoughts

Inversion of Control is a powerful architectural pattern that can greatly improve the quality and maintainability of our software projects. By allowing the framework to manage dependencies and control flow, we can focus on writing modular and reusable code, making our applications more flexible and adaptable to changes. It may require some effort to implement IoC in our projects, but the benefits it brings make it a valuable tool for any software engineer.

Chapter 30: Layered Architecture

Layered architecture is a software design pattern that breaks down the application into separate layers, each with its own specific responsibility. This approach adds a level of abstraction, making it easier to manage and maintain the code.

Explanation

The layered architecture pattern involves dividing an application into layers, each with a specific set of functions and responsibilities. These layers are stacked on top of each other, with each layer only able to interact with the layer directly below it. This creates a hierarchical structure, with each layer dependent on the layer below it.The most common layers in a layered architecture are the presentation layer, business logic layer, and data access layer. The presentation layer is responsible for handling the user interface, while the business logic layer handles the application's business rules and processes. The data access layer is responsible for handling data storage and retrieval.

Real-world Examples

Many popular applications and frameworks use layered architecture as their underlying software design. For example, Microsoft's .NET Framework uses a layered architecture to provide a foundation for building applications. The presentation layer is represented by the user interface, the business logic layer is made up of the language-neutral common language runtime, and the data access layer is managed by the ADO.NET technology.Another example is the Java Enterprise Edition (EE) platform, which also utilizes the layered architecture pattern. The web layer serves as the presentation layer, the EJB layer serves as the business logic layer, and the data layer is managed by the Java Persistence API (JPA).

Benefits

The layered architecture pattern offers several benefits, making it a popular choice for software design. One of the main advantages of layered architecture is its inherent scalability. As each layer only needs to interact with the layer directly below it, it helps to maintain a clean separation of concerns and allows for easy scaling as the application grows. Moreover, the layered architecture allows for easier testing and debugging, as each layer can be tested individually. This helps to identify and fix bugs more efficiently, making the application more robust and reliable. Additionally, using a layered architecture can improve software maintainability. As each layer has specific responsibilities, it makes it easier for developers to make changes or add new features without affecting the entire application's functionality.

In conclusion, the layered architecture pattern offers various benefits that make it an attractive choice for software design. By breaking down an application into layers, it adds an element of abstraction that simplifies complex systems and makes them easier to manage and maintain.

Chapter 31: Model-Driven Architecture

Definition

Model-Driven Architecture (MDA) is a software development approach that focuses on creating models as the primary means of design and development. It is based on the principle of separating the specification of system functionality from the implementation of this functionality. In other words, MDA allows developers to create high-level models of a system and use these models to automatically generate the necessary code for the system.The MDA approach is based on the Object Management Group's (OMG) Model-Driven Architecture (MDA) standard, which defines a set of specifications and tools for applying the MDA approach.

Implementation

The implementation of MDA involves the development of models using standardized modeling languages such as Unified Modeling Language (UML) or Business Process Model and Notation (BPMN). These models are then used to automatically generate code in a specific programming language, such as Java or C++, using code generation tools.The MDA approach also incorporates the use of model transformation, which allows for the transformation of one model into another at different levels of abstraction. This allows for the models to be refined and adjusted as needed, without having to start from scratch.

Benefits

The MDA approach offers a range of benefits for software development, including:

1. Improved Productivity
One of the key benefits of MDA is its ability to generate code from models, which significantly reduces the amount of manual coding required. This results in increased productivity and faster delivery of software products.

2. Increased Quality

Since MDA relies on high-level models, it allows for a more thorough and detailed design process. This results in better quality software that is less prone to errors and easier to maintain.

3. Higher Reusability

With MDA, models can be reused across different projects, reducing the need to repeat the same design and coding processes. This not only saves time but also improves consistency and reduces the likelihood of errors.

4. Scalability

The use of models in MDA allows for easier scaling of software systems. As the models can be refined and adjusted, it becomes simpler to add new functionality or make changes to existing functionality without disrupting the entire system.

5. Simpler Maintenance

Since software developed using MDA is based on models, any changes or updates can be made directly to the model, which automatically reflects in the generated code. This simplifies the maintenance process and reduces the likelihood of errors.

6. Enhanced Collaboration

MDA facilitates collaboration between developers and other stakeholders by providing a common language for system design and development. This makes it easier for all team members to understand and contribute to the software development process.

7. Cost Savings

By reducing the amount of manual coding required, MDA can significantly reduce the overall costs of software development. Additionally, the improved quality and scalability of MDA-based systems can lead to long-term cost savings for organizations.

In Conclusion

Model-Driven Architecture offers a structured and efficient approach to software development, enabling organizations to produce high-quality, scalable, and cost-effective solutions. By using standardized models and automated code generation, MDA allows developers to focus on the essential aspects of system design and development, resulting in faster delivery times and improved collaboration among team members. With the increasing complexity of software systems, the use of MDA can be a valuable tool for organizations looking to stay ahead in the rapidly evolving technology landscape.

Chapter 32: Aspect-Oriented Programming

Explanation

Aspect-oriented programming, commonly referred to as AOP, is an emerging software engineering paradigm that aims to address cross-cutting concerns in an efficient and manageable manner. It achieves this by allowing developers to modularize non-functional requirements, such as logging, error handling, security, and performance monitoring, into separate aspects. These aspects can then be easily woven into the main codebase, without the need for frequent code changes and duplication.AOP operates on the principle of separation of concerns, which is a fundamental principle of good software engineering. It promotes the concept of dividing a software system into smaller, well-defined parts, with each part focusing on a specific piece of functionality. This not only improves the maintainability of the system but also makes it easier to understand and modify in the future.

Use Cases

There are several use cases where aspect-oriented programming can be beneficial. One of the most common use cases is for implementing logging in a software system. With AOP, developers can define a logging aspect that will automatically capture and log relevant information from any method call, without the need for explicit logging statements in the main codebase. This not only reduces the amount of code that needs to be written but also ensures consistent and comprehensive logging across the entire system.Another use case where AOP can be useful is for implementing security measures. By defining a security aspect, developers can easily add authentication and authorization functionality to the system without modifying the core logic. This is particularly helpful in large systems where security requirements can change frequently, as it allows for easy modification without impacting the main codebase.

Advantages

One of the main advantages of aspect-oriented programming is improved modularity and flexibility. By separating non-functional concerns into aspects, developers can modify or add new functionality without impacting the rest of the system. This makes it easier to adapt to changing requirements and scale the system as needed. AOP also promotes code reuse. With aspects, developers can easily reuse code across different modules, reducing code duplication and increasing overall efficiency. This is particularly helpful in large systems with complex functionality, where certain aspects may be needed in multiple parts of the codebase. Another significant advantage of AOP is improved maintainability. Aspects allow developers to encapsulate cross-cutting concerns in a separate module, making it easier to locate and modify code related to specific functionalities. This not only improves the overall codebase but also saves time when it comes to debugging and troubleshooting issues. In addition, aspect-oriented programming promotes better code organization and readability. By separating concerns, developers can write cleaner and more maintainable code that is easier to understand. This not only benefits the current team but also makes it easier for future developers to join the project. Finally, AOP can improve system performance by reducing the number of log statements and error-handling code in the main codebase. With aspects, these functionalities can be optimized and managed separately, resulting in a leaner and more efficient system.As aspect-oriented programming continues to gain popularity, it is important for software engineers to understand its concepts and benefits. By utilizing this paradigm, developers can build more robust and maintainable software systems, leading to a better overall user experience.

Chapter 33: Behavior-Driven Development

If you are a software engineer looking for ways to improve your development process, then Behavior-Driven Development (BDD) is a concept that you should definitely explore. BDD is a methodology that emphasizes collaboration and communication between different stakeholders of a software project. It aims to bridge the gap between business requirements and technical implementation, resulting in high-quality software that meets the needs of both the end-users and the business. In this chapter, we will delve deeper into the world of Behavior-Driven Development and discuss its explanation, benefits, and best practices.

Explanation

Behavior-Driven Development is an approach to software development that has gained popularity in recent years. It is an evolution of Test-Driven Development (TDD) and follows a similar methodology: write tests before writing code. However, BDD differs from TDD in its focus on behavior rather than implementation details. The main goal of BDD is to define the behavior of a system through examples in a language that can be understood by all stakeholders, including developers, testers, and business analysts.BDD is based on the concept of "outside-in" development, where the customer's perspective is always kept in mind. This means that the focus is on delivering value to the end-users rather than just meeting technical requirements. In BDD, scenarios are defined using a format known as Given-When-Then. The Given clause sets up the initial context, the When clause describes the action being performed, and the Then clause defines the expected outcome. These scenarios serve as executable specifications for the system and are used to guide the development process.

Benefits

One of the main benefits of BDD is improved collaboration between different stakeholders. By using a common language to define the behavior of the system, developers and non-technical team members can better understand each other's perspectives. This results in a shared understanding of the requirements, leading to a more efficient development process. BDD also helps in identifying and preventing potential bugs early on in the development process. By writing tests before writing code, any issues or discrepancies in the requirements can be caught and resolved early, reducing the overall time and effort spent on debugging.Another advantage of BDD is its focus on delivering value to the end-users. By defining the system's behavior through examples, BDD ensures that the final product meets the user's needs and expectations. This leads to better user adoption and satisfaction, ultimately resulting in the success of the project.

Best Practices

To successfully implement BDD in your development process, here are some best practices that you should keep in mind:

1. Collaboration is key

BDD is a collaborative methodology, and it is essential to involve all stakeholders in the process. This includes developers, testers, business analysts, and even the end-users. By working together, the team can identify and address any issues or discrepancies in the requirements early on, leading to a smoother development process.

2. Keep it simple

One of the main principles of BDD is simplicity. Scenarios should be written in plain language that is easily understandable by all stakeholders. Avoid using technical terms or jargon, as this can lead to confusion and misinterpretation.

3. Focus on behavior, not implementation

As mentioned earlier, BDD is all about defining the behavior of the system, not the implementation details. Avoid getting caught up in technicalities and keep the focus on delivering value to the end-users.

4. Automate tests

To fully reap the benefits of BDD, it is essential to automate your tests. This allows for quicker feedback and makes it easier to catch and fix any issues that may arise.

5. Continuous collaboration and refinement

BDD is an iterative process, and it is essential to continuously collaborate and refine the scenarios as the project progresses. As new features are added or requirements change, the scenarios may need to be updated to reflect these changes.

In conclusion, Behavior-Driven Development is a powerful methodology that can greatly benefit software development processes. Its focus on collaboration, simplicity, and delivering value to the end-users makes it a valuable tool for any software engineer. By following best practices and understanding its benefits, you can effectively incorporate BDD into your development process and deliver high-quality software that meets the needs of both the business and its users.

Chapter 34: Test-Driven Development

Difference from TDD

Test-Driven Development (TDD) is an agile software development approach where automated tests are written before writing the actual code. It involves creating small, focused tests that guide the development process and help ensure the code is functioning correctly. TDD is different from traditional testing methods because it focuses on writing tests before the code, rather than after. This allows for a more structured and disciplined approach to software development, as well as a higher level of code coverage.One of the key differences between TDD and traditional testing methods is that TDD is a cycle, rather than a one-time event. In traditional testing, developers write the code first and then test it afterwards. However, in TDD, tests are written first, then the code is written to pass the tests, and then the code is refactored. This cycle is repeated continuously throughout the development process. This approach allows for quick feedback and adjustments, leading to a more efficient and streamlined development process.

Implementation Steps

Implementing TDD requires a change in mindset and a learning curve for many developers. However, with practice and dedication, TDD can greatly improve the quality and maintainability of code. Here are the basic steps involved in implementing TDD:

1. Write a failing test: The first step in TDD is to write a test that simulates the behavior of the code you want to write but does not yet exist. This test will fail since the code does not exist yet.

2. Write the simplest code that passes the test: Once there is a failing test, the next step is to write the simplest code that would make the test pass. This code does not have to be perfect, as it will be continuously refactored.

3. Refactor the code: Once the test passes, the code needs to be refactored to improve

its quality and maintainability. This step is crucial in TDD as it ensures that the code stays clean and efficient.

4. Repeat: The cycle then repeats, with a new failing test, simple code, and refactoring. This process is repeated continuously throughout the development process.

Real-world Examples

TDD has been adopted by many software development companies, both large and small, across a wide range of industries. Here are some real-world examples of companies that have successfully implemented TDD:

1. Amazon: Amazon, the multinational technology company, is known for its successful implementation of TDD. They use TDD to ensure the quality and reliability of their online shopping platform, as well as their cloud computing services.

2. Netflix: The popular streaming service Netflix also implements TDD in their development process. They use TDD to test their code and ensure that their platform runs smoothly, delivering a seamless user experience.

3. Microsoft: Microsoft is another company that has embraced TDD in their software development process. They use TDD to continuously test their code and ensure that their products, such as Microsoft Office and Windows, are of top-notch quality.

4. Google: Google, the multinational technology company, also follows TDD principles in their development process. They use TDD to test their code and ensure the reliability of their search engine, as well as their wide range of software products.TDD has proven to be a valuable and effective approach to software development, with many companies reaping the benefits of its implementation. It not only leads to better quality code but also helps reduce development time and costs. As TDD continues to gain popularity and recognition in the software engineering world, it is safe to say that it is here to stay.

Chapter 35: Domain-Driven Design

Explanation

Domain-Driven Design (DDD) is an approach to software development that focuses on building software based on a deep understanding of the business domain. It is a philosophy that puts the domain at the center of the development process, rather than being an afterthought. The premise of DDD is that by understanding the domain, the code and design of a software system can better align with business needs. It was first introduced by Eric Evans in his book "Domain-Driven Design: Tackling Complexity in the Heart of Software" in 2003 and has since gained widespread popularity in the software engineering community.

Benefits

One of the main benefits of DDD is that it helps reduce complexity in software design. By focusing on the domain, developers can identify core business rules and model them accordingly, leading to a more logical and maintainable codebase. This also enables easier communication between developers and stakeholders, as they can use the same language to discuss business requirements and technical implementation. Another advantage of DDD is that it promotes a strategic approach to software development. Instead of just building features and functionalities, developers can align their code with the business goals of the project. This can lead to a more valuable and impactful product, leading to higher customer satisfaction and business success.Moreover, DDD helps in identifying areas of the code that are critical to the business and require more attention. By focusing on these core components, developers can ensure the stability and reliability of the software. This can also result in cost savings as the team can prioritize their efforts on the most essential parts of the code.

Implementation

Implementing DDD requires a deep understanding of the business domain. Developers must work closely with domain experts, such as product managers and business analysts, to gain a thorough understanding of the business and its goals. This can be achieved through discussions, workshops, and domain modeling exercises. Once the domain is fully understood, the next step is to identify and define the core domain concepts. These are the key elements that make up the business and are essential for the software to function. The development team can then create models based on these concepts, such as entities, value objects, and aggregates, to represent the business logic in code. Another crucial aspect of DDD is the concept of bounded contexts. This refers to the idea that different parts of the codebase may have different models and terminology, based on their specific purposes. By defining the scope and boundaries of each bounded context, developers can avoid confusion and ensure the consistency and integrity of the code. In addition to the technical aspects, DDD also requires a shift in mindset and communication within the development team. Developers must have a clear understanding of the business and work collaboratively to build a software system that meets the needs of the domain. Regular communication and feedback between the team and stakeholders are also crucial for successful implementation of DDD.

In conclusion, Domain-Driven Design is a powerful approach to software development that prioritizes understanding the business domain and aligning it with the technical aspects of a project. By using DDD, developers can reduce complexity, create more valuable products, and ultimately deliver successful and impactful software solutions.

Chapter 36: Test Automation

Whether you are a seasoned software engineer or just starting out in the world of code, test automation is a crucial aspect of ensuring the quality and reliability of any software product. In this chapter, we will delve into the definition, types, and best practices of test automation, shedding light on the importance and benefits of incorporating it into your development process.

Definition

Test automation, also known as automated testing, is the process of automating the execution of test cases, using specialized tools or scripts, to assess the functionality and performance of a software product. This eliminates the need for manual intervention, making the testing process more efficient, accurate, and less time-consuming. Automated testing involves running a set of predefined test cases or scripts against the software product to check for any bugs, errors, and deviations from the expected behavior. It is an integral part of the quality assurance process and helps in identifying issues at an early stage of development, reducing the overall cost and time of bug fixing.

Types

There are various types of test automation that can be used depending on the specific needs and requirements of a software project. Some of the commonly used types are:

Unit Testing

This type of testing involves evaluating the individual units or components of a software product, such as classes, methods, functions, etc. It helps in ensuring that each unit performs as expected and is suitable for integration with other units.

Integration Testing

Integration testing involves testing the integration and interaction between different units or modules of a software product. It helps in identifying any compatibility issues between components and ensures the overall stability and functionality of the entire system.

Functional Testing

This type of testing is focused on verifying the functionality of a software product and ensuring that it meets the specified requirements. It involves running test cases to check if the features and functionalities of the software are working as expected.

Performance Testing

Performance testing is used to assess the speed, scalability, and stability of a software product under different load conditions. It helps in identifying any performance bottlenecks and ensuring that the software can handle a large number of users or data without any issues.

User Acceptance Testing

User acceptance testing (UAT) is performed to check if a software product meets the expectations of end-users and is ready to be released into the market. It involves running test cases from the user's perspective and helps in gaining valuable feedback and insights.

Best Practices

While test automation can undoubtedly improve the efficiency and effectiveness of the testing process, there are certain best practices that should be followed for optimal results. Some of these practices include:

Identify the Right Test Cases

Not all tests can be automated, and it is essential to identify the types of tests that are best suited for automation. Prioritize the most critical and frequently performed tests and automate them first to yield the maximum benefit.

Incorporate Test Automation into the Development Process

Test automation should be an integral part of the development process and not an afterthought. It is crucial to start automating tests from the early stages of development and continue to do so throughout the cycle to catch bugs and issues at the earliest.

Use Quality Tools

Choosing the right automation tool is crucial for the success of your testing efforts. Evaluate different options and select a reliable tool that offers the necessary features and supports the programming language and platforms used for the product.

Don't Forget Maintenance

Test automation requires continuous maintenance, and it is essential to keep updating and improving the test cases as the software product evolves. Regular review and upkeep of the test suite can help in keeping the tests relevant and efficient.

Collaborate and Communicate

Effective communication and collaboration between team members involved in testing and development are vital for the success of test automation. It is essential to ensure that the testing efforts align with the development goals and any significant changes are communicated to all team members.

In conclusion, test automation is incredibly beneficial for any software engineering project, and its importance cannot be understated. It improves the quality and reliability of the software product, reduces the time and cost of testing, and allows for early detection and bug fixing. By understanding the types and best practices of test automation, software engineers can make better-informed decisions and deliver high-quality products that meet user expectations.

Chapter 37: Continuous Integration

Explanation

Continuous Integration is a software development practice that allows teams to constantly integrate code changes into a shared repository, enabling them to identify and resolve conflicts early on. This process involves automating the build, testing, and integration of code changes, ensuring that the final product is always in a working state.

Benefits

Continuous Integration offers numerous benefits to software engineers and development teams. Firstly, it reduces the risk of conflicts and errors in the codebase, as any issues are identified and resolved quickly during the integration process. This leads to a more stable and functional final product. Additionally, Continuous Integration allows for faster delivery of software updates, as code changes are constantly being integrated and tested. This leads to a more agile development process and enables teams to respond to customer needs and market demands more efficiently.Moreover, Continuous Integration promotes collaboration among team members as they are constantly working together to integrate code changes and resolve conflicts. This creates a sense of ownership and responsibility towards the project, resulting in a more cohesive team and a better end product.

Tools

There are various tools available to assist with implementing Continuous Integration in software engineering. Some popular options include Jenkins, Travis CI, CircleCI, and TeamCity. These tools offer features such as automated testing, code quality checks, and integration with version control systems. Apart from these tools, there are also various add-ons and plugins that can enhance the Continuous Integration process and integrate with other development tools. For example, some tools offer integrations with project management tools, allowing for better communication and visibility of project progress. Furthermore, many companies offer their own proprietary tools for Continuous Integration, tailored to their specific development processes and needs. These tools often offer more advanced features and flexibility, but also come at a cost. It is essential for software engineers to carefully evaluate and choose the right tool for their project, as it can greatly impact the effectiveness and efficiency of their Continuous Integration process.

In conclusion, Continuous Integration is a crucial practice in the world of software engineering. It enables teams to constantly integrate and test code changes, leading to a stable and functional end product. With the right tools and processes in place, Continuous Integration can greatly enhance the development process and contribute to the success of a project.

Chapter 38: Quality Assurance - The Key to a Successful Software Development Process

Quality assurance is a crucial aspect of any software development process. It involves a series of measures and techniques that are implemented to ensure that the final product meets the highest standards of quality. In the ever-evolving and fast-paced world of software engineering, where new technologies and methodologies are constantly emerging, it is imperative to have robust quality assurance processes in place.

SOLID: Building a Strong Foundation for Quality Assurance

When it comes to software development, the SOLID principles are the pillars of a strong and sustainable foundation. These principles, coined by Robert C. Martin in the early 2000s, stand for Single Responsibility, Open-Closed, Liskov Substitution, Interface Segregation, and Dependency Inversion. These principles, although simple in concept, have a significant impact on the quality of the software being developed. The Single Responsibility principle states that every module or class should have a single responsibility, and that responsibility should be entirely encapsulated within that module or class. This helps to reduce the complexity of the codebase and makes it easier to maintain and extend the software in the future. By following this principle, the code becomes less prone to bugs and easier to test, thus improving the overall quality of the software. The Open-Closed principle states that software entities should be open for extension, but closed for modification. In simpler terms, this means that the code should be designed in a way that allows for new features to be added without modifying the existing code. This helps to ensure that changes made to the software do not inadvertently introduce bugs or affect the existing functionality, thus maintaining the quality of the codebase. The Liskov Substitution principle states that objects in a program should be replaceable with instances of their subtypes without affecting the correctness of the program. This principle ensures that the code is written in a way where any child class can be used in place of the parent class without changing the behavior of the program. By following this principle, the codebase becomes more flexible and extensible, ultimately leading to a higher quality of the software.

The Interface Segregation principle states that clients should not be forced to depend on interfaces that they do not use. In simpler terms, this means that interfaces should be small and specific to the needs of the client, rather than having one large interface that caters to multiple clients. This helps to reduce the coupling between objects and makes it easier to maintain and test the code, thus improving the quality of the software.The Dependency Inversion principle states that high-level modules should not depend on low-level modules. Instead, both should depend on abstractions. This helps to reduce the interdependence between classes and modules, thus making the codebase more maintainable and extensible. By following this principle, the code becomes more flexible, which ultimately leads to a higher quality of the software.

DRY: Don't Repeat Yourself - A Mantra for Consistency and Quality

The DRY principle, which stands for Don't Repeat Yourself, is another critical aspect of quality assurance in software development. It is a basic programming principle that promotes the idea of reducing repetition and redundancy in code. When a codebase follows this principle, it becomes easier to maintain, test and extend, ultimately leading to a higher quality of software.When code is repeated in multiple places, it not only increases the chances of bugs and errors but also makes it harder to change in the future. This leads to a lack of consistency in the codebase, which can affect the overall quality of the software. By following the DRY principle, developers are encouraged to reuse existing code rather than repeating it, thus promoting consistency and reducing the chances of errors.

YAGNI: You Ain't Gonna Need It - Minimizing Waste, Maximizing Quality

The YAGNI principle, which stands for You Ain't Gonna Need It, is another essential aspect of quality assurance in software development. It is a principle that promotes the idea of minimizing waste by only implementing what is currently needed, rather than trying to predict future requirements. By following this principle, developers can focus on building the necessary features and improving their quality, rather than wasting time and resources on features that may never be needed.Often, developers tend to over-engineer features and functionality, anticipating future requirements that may never even arise. This leads to an increase in complexity and a decrease in the quality of the software. By following the YAGNI principle, developers are encouraged to only implement what is currently needed, thus reducing waste and improving the overall quality of the software.

The Role of Quality Assurance in the Software Development Process

Now that we have a deeper understanding of the key principles that contribute to the quality of software, let's explore the role of quality assurance in the software development process. Quality Assurance, often referred to as QA, is an integral part of the software development lifecycle, where it plays a significant role in ensuring the final product meets the desired level of quality. The primary goal of quality assurance is to identify and eliminate defects or discrepancies in the software before it is released to the end-users. It involves a series of processes that are designed to test and validate the software, starting from the requirements gathering phase all the way through to the final release. These processes can include functional testing, unit testing, integration testing, user acceptance testing, and more.Additionally, quality assurance also involves reviewing and improving the codebase by following industry best practices and standards. This can include conducting code reviews, ensuring proper coding conventions are followed, and implementing automated testing strategies. By following these practices, quality assurance helps to identify and fix bugs early on in the development process, thus reducing the chances of costly rework in the future.

The Benefits of a Strong Quality Assurance Process

A robust quality assurance process has numerous benefits for both the development team and the end-users. Firstly, it helps to ensure that the software meets the desired level of quality, thus reducing the chances of bugs and errors. This, in turn, leads to improved customer satisfaction, trust, and loyalty towards the product. Secondly, a strong quality assurance process helps to identify and fix bugs in the early stages of development, which ultimately reduces the overall cost of the project. By catching and fixing bugs early on, development teams can avoid costly rework and delays, thus keeping projects within budget and on schedule.Thirdly, a strong quality assurance process promotes consistency in the codebase, making it easier to maintain and extend the software in the future. By consistently following coding standards and best practices, developers can ensure that the codebase remains manageable and scalable, thus reducing redevelopment costs and increasing the lifespan of the software.

In Conclusion

Quality assurance is an essential aspect of software development that should never be overlooked. By following the principles of SOLID, DRY, and YAGNI, developers can build a strong and sustainable foundation that promotes consistency, reduces waste, and improves the overall quality of the software. With a robust quality assurance process in place, developers can ensure that the end-users receive a high-quality product that meets their expectations and exceeds their needs.

Chapter 39: Refactoring

Refactoring, also known as code refactoring, is the process of restructuring existing code without changing its external behavior. It is an essential aspect of software development that helps improve the quality and maintainability of code. Refactoring is not just about making code "look pretty," but rather taking a step back and seeing the bigger picture of the codebase. It involves analyzing the structure, design patterns, and organization of code to ensure that it follows best practices and is in line with the overall project goals.

Definition

Refactoring is a systematic process of making code more efficient, maintainable, and extensible without altering its functionality. It involves making small, incremental changes to the codebase without rewriting it from scratch. This allows developers to continuously improve the code's design and structure, leading to better performance, readability, and scalability. Refactoring is an ongoing process throughout the development lifecycle, as codebases continually evolve and new features are added.

Techniques

There are various techniques involved in refactoring, with each serving a specific purpose. One of the most common techniques is the "extract method," which involves separating a section of code into its own method. This helps improve code readability, reduces code duplication, and promotes reuse. Another popular technique is "rename," where variables, methods, or classes are renamed to have more meaningful and descriptive names, making the code easier to understand.Other techniques include "extract variable," "inline variable," "move method," "inline method," "replace conditional logic with polymorphism," and many more. Each of these techniques serves a specific purpose in improving the code's structure and following best practices.

Best Practices

Refactoring can be a daunting and time-consuming process if not done correctly. Therefore, it is essential to follow some best practices to ensure that refactoring is carried out effectively. First and foremost, refactoring should be done in small, incremental steps so that the codebase is not broken at any point. It is also crucial to have a solid test suite in place to ensure that the refactored code still functions correctly. It is also recommended to use version control systems such as Git to track changes made during refactoring. This allows developers to revert to previous versions of the code if needed. Refactoring should also be done in collaboration with other team members to ensure consistency and prevent conflicts.Another important best practice is to prioritize refactoring based on the project's needs. Not all code requires refactoring, and it is essential to focus on areas of code that are used frequently, contain bugs, or are difficult to understand.

Conclusion

In conclusion, refactoring is a key aspect of software engineering that helps improve code quality, readability, and maintainability. It involves making small, incremental changes to the codebase using various techniques to ensure that it follows best practices. By continuously refactoring code, developers can not only improve the current codebase but also set a foundation for future development and scalability. So, make sure to prioritize refactoring and incorporate it as a regular practice in your software development process.

Chapter 40: Performance Optimization

In the fast-paced world of software engineering, performance is key. Users expect applications and systems to run smoothly and quickly without any delays or errors. That is why performance optimization is crucial for any successful software project. In this chapter, we will delve into the purpose, benefits and best practices of performance optimization, helping you understand how to create high-performing software that delights users.

Purpose

The purpose of performance optimization is to improve the speed, responsiveness and efficiency of a software system or application. It involves identifying and addressing bottlenecks, code inefficiencies and other factors that may be slowing down the system. By optimizing performance, developers can ensure that their software is able to handle high volumes of data and requests, while providing a seamless user experience.

Benefits

The benefits of performance optimization are numerous and can have a significant impact on the success of a software project. Here are just a few of the major benefits that come with optimizing performance:

1. Enhanced User Experience
In today's competitive market, users have high expectations when it comes to software performance. Slow and unresponsive applications can be a major turn-off and cause users to abandon the software altogether. By optimizing performance, developers can ensure that their software runs smoothly and efficiently, providing a positive user experience and keeping users engaged.

2. Improved Efficiency
Performance optimization often involves making changes to code and processes that can lead to a more efficient system. This can save valuable time and resources,

allowing developers to focus on creating new features and functionality instead of constantly fixing performance issues.

3. Cost Savings

Optimizing performance can also result in cost savings for organizations. By creating efficient and streamlined systems, developers can reduce the hardware and infrastructure requirements, saving the company money in the long run.

4. Better Scalability

As software usage grows, the demands on the system increase. Performance optimization allows for better scalability, meaning that the software can handle larger volumes of data and requests without sacrificing speed and efficiency. This is especially important for applications and systems that need to support a large user base.

Best Practices

Optimizing performance is not a one-time task; it requires constant monitoring and improvement. Here are some best practices to keep in mind when approaching performance optimization:

1. Set Performance Goals

Before beginning any performance optimization efforts, it is essential to define measurable performance goals. This could include response time, throughput, or any other relevant metrics. These goals will serve as a benchmark for measuring the success of performance optimization efforts.

2. Identify and Address Bottlenecks

The first step in optimization is to identify any bottlenecks in the system. This could include database queries, network calls, or inefficient code. By pinpointing the bottleneck, developers can focus on improving specific areas to enhance overall performance.

3. Profile and Test Regularly

Profiling is the process of analyzing the performance of a system and identifying areas that could be improved. It is crucial to profile and test regularly to catch performance issues early on and make continuous improvements.

4. Optimize Code and Processes

Optimizing code and processes involves making changes to improve efficiency and performance. This could include optimizing database queries, reducing network communication, or using caching mechanisms. It is important to consider the specific needs of the system and make targeted optimizations to achieve the best results.

5. Utilize Performance Tools

There are many tools available that can help with performance optimization, such as profilers, load testing tools, and code analyzers. These tools can provide valuable insights into the performance of the system and help developers identify areas for improvement.

6. Monitor and Analyze Performance

After making performance optimizations, it is essential to continue monitoring and analyzing the system's performance to ensure that the changes have had the desired effect. This will also help to identify any new bottlenecks that may have arisen.

In conclusion, performance optimization is a vital aspect of software development that is often overlooked. By understanding its purpose, benefits, and best practices, developers can create high-performing software that meets user expectations and drives success for the application or system. Through continuous monitoring and improvement, performance optimization can ensure that software runs smoothly and efficiently, keeping users happy and engaged. So, make sure to prioritize performance optimization in your software projects, and watch your applications soar to new heights!

Chapter 41: Debugging Techniques

Debugging is an essential skill for any software engineer. It is the process of identifying and resolving errors or bugs within a software system. These bugs can range from simple syntax errors to complex logic issues that can be difficult to uncover. Debugging requires a combination of methods, tools, and best practices to effectively find and fix bugs.

Methods

There are several methods that can be used to debug code. These methods can vary depending on the type of bug and the complexity of the software system. Some common methods include:

1. Manual Debugging:
This method involves manually inspecting and tracing through the code to identify the source of the bug. It requires a deep understanding of the code and can be time-consuming and tedious.

2. Print Statements:
This method involves inserting print statements throughout the code to track the execution flow and identify the values of variables at different stages. It can be useful for simple bugs but can be overwhelming for complex systems.

3. Step-through Debugging:
Many Integrated Development Environments (IDEs) offer a step-through debugging feature. It allows programmers to execute the code line by line and examine the value of variables at each step. This method can be useful for complex bugs and can save time compared to manual debugging.

4. Profiling:
Profiling is a method of collecting data about the execution of a software system to identify bottlenecks and performance issues. It can help identify the source of bugs that are related to performance.

Tools

There are various tools available to aid in debugging. These tools can provide valuable information and can save time when trying to identify and fix bugs. Some commonly used debugging tools include:

1. Debuggers:
Debuggers are software tools that help programmers step through code and track variables and values. They provide a graphical representation of the execution flow and can help identify the source of the bug.

2. Logging Tools:
Logging tools allow programmers to insert logs at different stages of the code to track the execution flow and variable values. These logs can be viewed later to identify any issues or bugs.

3. Memory Analyzers:
Memory analyzers help identify issues related to memory management, such as memory leaks and heap overflows. These tools provide a graphical representation of memory usage and can help identify the location of the bug.

4. Code Coverage Tools:
Code coverage tools track the lines of code that are executed during the testing process. They can help identify any areas of the code that are not covered by tests, which can be potential areas for bugs.

Best Practices

Debugging is not just about using the right methods and tools; it also requires some best practices to be effective. Some best practices for debugging include:

1. Reproducing the Bug:
Before attempting to fix a bug, it is essential to try and reproduce it consistently. This can help ensure that the fix actually solves the problem and does not create new bugs.

2. Isolate the Bug:
When debugging, it is essential to isolate the bug and not make any unnecessary

changes to the code. This can help prevent inadvertently introducing new bugs and can make it easier to track the source of the issue.

3. Divide and Conquer:
When faced with a complex bug, it can be helpful to divide the code into smaller sections and test each section individually. This can help narrow down the source of the bug and make it easier to fix.

4. Use Version Control:
It is crucial to use version control for software projects to track changes and revert to previous versions if necessary. This can be helpful when attempting to fix a bug that may have been introduced in a recent code change.

In Conclusion

Debugging is an essential skill for software engineers and requires a combination of methods, tools, and best practices to be effective. It is a process that can be time-consuming, but with the right approach, it can save time and frustration in the long run. By following best practices and using the right tools, software engineers can effectively identify and fix bugs, leading to a more efficient and reliable software system. So remember, when faced with a bug, don't get discouraged. Keep calm and debug on!

Chapter 42: Strategies for Effective Software Debugging

Debugging is a crucial aspect of software engineering. It is the process of identifying and fixing errors in a program, and it is an inevitable part of the software development lifecycle. However, with the increasing complexity and scale of modern software systems, debugging has become a challenging task. According to a survey, on average, developers spend around 50% of their time debugging code. This indicates the critical role that debugging plays in successful software development.In this chapter, we will discuss some effective strategies, tools, and best practices for debugging software. These techniques will not only help you save time and effort but also improve the overall quality of your code. So, let's dive into the world of debugging and explore some useful tips and tricks.

Strategies

1. Start with a Plan: As a software engineer, it is essential to have a systematic approach to debugging. Rushing into fixing bugs without a proper plan can lead to wasting time and effort. Start by analyzing the problem, understanding its root cause, and then come up with a plan of action.

2. Divide and Conquer: When faced with a complex bug, it can be overwhelming to try and fix the entire problem at once. Instead, break down the issue into smaller parts, and then tackle them individually. This approach will make debugging more manageable and help you pinpoint the root cause more effectively.

3. Use Debugging Tools: There are various debugging tools available in the market that can help you identify and fix errors in your code. These tools have features like code stepping, breakpoints, and data inspection, which can assist you in understanding the flow of your program and identifying the source of the bug.

4. Leverage Test Cases: Test cases are invaluable when it comes to debugging. They can help you recreate the problem in a controlled environment and narrow down the issue's cause. It is important to have a comprehensive test suite that covers all aspects

of the software to ensure efficient debugging.

5. Collaborate with Your Team: Debugging can be a team effort. In complex and large-scale projects, getting another set of eyes to look at the code can be beneficial. Your team members might bring a fresh perspective or suggest a different approach to solving the bug that you might have overlooked.

Tools

1. Integrated Development Environment (IDE): IDEs like Visual Studio, Eclipse, and IntelliJ have built-in debugging tools that allow you to step through your code, set breakpoints, and inspect data. These tools work seamlessly with the code editor, making it easier to debug in real-time.

2. Version Control Systems (VCS): VCSs like Git, Mercurial, and SVN are not just for managing code versions. They also come with handy features that can help you track and fix bugs. With VCS, you can roll back to a previous working version of your code, compare changes, and collaborate with your team to fix bugs.

3. Automated Debugging Tools: There are various automated debugging tools available that can save you time and effort. These tools use machine learning and artificial intelligence to analyze your code and suggest possible bugs or performance issues. They can help you find errors that you might have missed during manual debugging.

Best Practices

1. Write Readable Code: Writing code that is easy to read and understand is essential. It not only makes debugging easier but also improves the overall maintainability of your code. Use meaningful variable names, comments, and follow coding standards to make your code more readable.

2. Use Exception Handling: Exception handling is a useful technique that can help you manage errors in your code. Catching and handling exceptions can prevent your program from crashing or generating unanticipated errors, making it easier to debug.

3. Keep an Error Log: Keeping track of the bugs you encounter can be useful in identifying patterns and common issues in your code. Make it a practice to maintain an error log that includes the bug description, the steps to reproduce it, and how it was resolved. This log can also serve as a reference for future debugging.

4. Document Your Code: Documenting your code can save you a lot of time and effort while debugging. It acts as a guide to understanding the code's functionality and can help you track changes made by other team members. Use a tool like Doxygen to generate documentation automatically from the code.

Chapter 43: Version Control Systems

Whether you are a solo developer working on a personal project or a large team collaborating on a complex software system, keeping track of changes made to your code is essential. This is where version control systems come into play. They provide a way to track and manage changes to your code, making collaboration and development processes more efficient and organized.

Explanation

Version control systems, also known as source code management systems, are tools that manage changes to source code, documents, and other files. They provide a way to track and compare different versions of a file, which is crucial for software development projects with multiple contributors.The core functionality of a version control system is its ability to track and store changes made to code files. Each time a change is made, the system creates a new version of the file, allowing users to roll back to previous versions if needed. This is especially useful in case of bugs or errors introduced in the code.

Common Features

While different version control systems may have varying features and functionalities, there are some common features that most of them provide:

1. History Tracking

One of the most crucial features of version control systems is the ability to track changes made to a file over time. This includes both the content and structure of the file, allowing users to see what was changed, when, and by whom. This history is especially useful for tracking down bugs or finding specific versions of a file.

2. Branching and Merging

Branching is the process of creating a new version of a codebase that is separate from the main branch. This allows developers to work on new features or experiment without affecting the main codebase. When the changes from the branch are ready, they can be merged back into the main branch, incorporating the changes into the codebase. This feature is essential for collaboration and managing different versions of a project.

3. Collaboration

Most version control systems offer features that support collaboration among team members. This includes the ability to work on the same codebase, track changes made by different contributors and resolve conflicts in case of overlapping changes.

4. Code Reviews

Code reviews are a crucial aspect of software development, and many version control systems offer built-in tools for conducting code reviews. These tools allow team members to provide feedback and suggestions for improving code quality, improving overall collaboration and codebase health.

Pros and Cons

As with any tool or technology, there are both advantages and disadvantages to using version control systems.

Pros:

- Efficient Collaboration: Version control systems make collaboration among team members more efficient by providing tools for tracking changes, resolving conflicts, and merging code.

- Clear Version History: The ability to track changes made to a file over time allows for clear and organized version history, making it easier to spot bugs or roll back to a previous version if needed.

- Code Reviews: Many version control systems provide built-in tools for conducting code reviews, which can significantly improve code quality and collaboration among team members.

- Backup and Recovery: Version control systems act as a backup for your codebase, ensuring that changes are not lost and can be recovered if necessary.

Cons:

- Learning Curve: Version control systems can be complex and may have a steep learning curve for beginners.

- Maintenance: Setting up and maintaining a version control system might require some time and effort, especially for larger projects.

- Dependency on Tools: Using a version control system means you are dependent on a specific tool or software, which may cause issues if the system malfunctions or becomes obsolete in the future.

In Conclusion

Version control systems are an essential tool for modern software development, providing a way to track, manage, and collaborate on changes made to source code. While they may have a learning curve, their benefits far outweigh any potential drawbacks, making them a valuable asset for any software engineering project. Whether you are working solo or in a team, using a version control system can significantly improve your development processes and lead to better, more efficient code.

Chapter 44: Exploring the Future of Software Engineering through Agile Methodologies

Software engineering is a constantly evolving field, with new technologies and methodologies emerging at a rapid pace. In order to keep up with the ever-changing landscape, software engineers must continuously adapt and evolve their practices. One such adaptation is the use of Agile methodologies, which have gained popularity in recent years due to their focus on collaboration, flexibility, and efficiency. In this chapter, we will delve into the world of Agile and its various methodologies, starting with the most widely used: Scrum, Kanban, and Extreme Programming.

Scrum: The Art of Collaboration

Scrum is an Agile framework that emphasizes collaboration, iteration, and constant communication among team members. It relies on a product owner, a Scrum master, and a development team working in close collaboration to deliver working software in short iterations called sprints. This approach allows for continuous feedback, constant re-evaluation, and quick adaptation to changing requirements.One of the key principles of Scrum is the use of a product backlog, a prioritized list of features and user stories that need to be implemented. The team then selects a subset of items from the backlog to work on during a sprint, with the goal of delivering a working product increment by the end of each sprint. This approach not only ensures a steady flow of deliverables but also encourages frequent collaboration and communication among team members.

Kanban: The Art of Visualization

Kanban is another popular Agile methodology that focuses on visualizing work, limiting work in progress, and promoting continuous improvement. Kanban utilizes a Kanban board, which is a visualization tool that enables teams to see the status of each task and visualize the flow of work. This promotes greater transparency and encourages team members to work collaboratively to address any bottlenecks or impediments that may arise.Kanban also emphasizes the importance of limiting work in progress (WIP) to avoid overloading team members and ensure a steady flow of work. This not only helps prevent burnout but also helps in identifying potential issues or blockers early on, allowing the team to address them before they become major problems.

Extreme Programming (XP): The Art of Quality

Extreme Programming (XP) is an Agile methodology that focuses on delivering high-quality software through constant testing and continuous integration. It advocates for practices such as pair programming, test-driven development, and refactoring, which promote collaboration, code quality, and the ability to adapt to changing requirements.Pair programming, or the practice of two programmers working together on the same code, not only helps in catching errors early on but also promotes knowledge sharing and collaboration. Test-driven development, where tests are written before the code is written, ensures that all code is thoroughly tested and integrates well with the existing codebase. And refactoring, or the continuous improvement of code, helps in keeping the codebase clean, maintainable, and adaptable to change.

The Future of Agile Methodologies

As the software engineering landscape continues to evolve, so too will the Agile methodologies that support it. In fact, we are already seeing the emergence of new methodologies such as Lean and Design Thinking, which build upon the principles of Agile and adapt them for specific industries and contexts. The future of Agile methodologies also lies in their integration with emerging technologies such as artificial intelligence and blockchain. These technologies have the potential to enhance collaboration, efficiency, and problem-solving capabilities, making them a natural fit for Agile methodologies.

In conclusion, Agile methodologies have significantly changed the way we approach software development, and they will continue to do so in the future. As the demand for faster, more efficient, and collaborative software development grows, so too will the need for Agile methodologies. It is crucial for software engineers to continue exploring and embracing these methodologies, adapting them to fit their needs and the rapidly evolving world of software development. As the saying goes, "change is the only constant," and Agile methodologies provide the perfect framework for embracing and thriving in this ever-changing landscape.

Chapter 45: Waterfall Model: The Pros and Cons

The Waterfall Model is one of the oldest approaches to software development and has been around since the 1960s. It follows a sequential design process in which each phase of development must be completed before moving on to the next. In this chapter, we will take a closer look at the pros and cons of using the Waterfall Model for software development.

Pros

Creative Freedom:
In the Waterfall Model, each phase of development is completed before moving on to the next. This allows for a clear understanding of the project requirements and gives developers the freedom to work on each phase without any interruptions or changes. This also encourages creativity and innovation in the development phase.

Maintains Timelines:
The Waterfall Model follows a structured and sequential approach, making it easier to estimate and manage timelines. This is especially beneficial for large-scale projects with a longer development time. Clients can also have a clear idea of when to expect the final product, making it easier for them to plan and make decisions.

Easy to Understand:
The Waterfall Model follows a linear approach, making it easy to understand for both developers and clients. This ensures transparency and clear communication between all stakeholders, making it less likely for misunderstandings or misinterpretations to occur.

Cons

Changes in Requirements:
The Waterfall Model is not ideal for projects where the client's requirements are not clearly defined. Since each phase must be completed before moving on to the next, any changes in the requirements can prove to be problematic and require going back to

previous phases, causing delays and additional costs.

High Risk:
Because the Waterfall Model follows a sequential approach, there is a higher risk of failure if any issues arise during the development process. This is especially true for large-scale projects with longer timelines, as it may be challenging to identify and rectify issues at an early stage.

Not Agile-friendly:
The Waterfall Model does not support frequent changes or iterations, making it unsuitable for projects that require an Agile approach. Any changes or additions must be carefully planned and implemented, which can slow down the development process and limit the agility of the project.

Use Cases and Limitations of the Waterfall Model

Use Cases

The Waterfall Model is most suitable for large-scale projects with well-defined and stable requirements. This approach is often used in government projects, where timelines and budgets are strictly defined, and changes in requirements are less likely to occur. It can also be useful for projects with a clear and fixed scope, as it allows for easy estimation of timelines and costs.

Limitations

The Waterfall Model is not ideal for complex and innovative projects, where changes and iterations are expected. It can also be challenging for clients to understand and visualize the final product until the later stages of development, which may lead to dissatisfaction or disappointment. Additionally, the linear approach of the Waterfall Model does not allow for testing and feedback until the end of the development cycle, increasing the risk of delivering a product that does not meet the client's expectations.

Conclusion

Overall, the Waterfall Model can be a useful approach for certain projects, but it has its limitations. It offers structure and ease of understanding, making it a popular choice for government and large-scale projects. However, it may not be the best fit for complex and innovative projects that require flexibility and frequent iterations. It's essential to weigh the pros and cons and consider the project's specific requirements before deciding to use the Waterfall Model for software development.

Chapter 46: Software Development Life Cycle

Software development is not a one-time event but an ongoing process that requires careful planning, execution, and evaluation. This is where the Software Development Life Cycle (SDLC) comes in. It is a systematic approach to developing software, which ensures that the end product is of high quality, meets user requirements, and is delivered on time and within budget.

Stages

The SDLC consists of several stages, each with its own set of activities and deliverables. These stages may vary depending on the methodology used by the development team, but the core principles remain the same.

1. Planning

This is the initial stage of the SDLC, where the project team identifies the scope, objectives, and timelines of the software development project. It involves conducting feasibility studies, defining requirements, and creating a project plan that outlines the resources, methods, and tools required for successful project completion.

2. Analysis

In this stage, the project team gathers and analyzes the requirements of the software product. This may involve conducting surveys, interviews, and focus groups with stakeholders and end-users. The goal is to identify the needs and expectations of the product's target audience and translate them into specific functional and non-functional requirements.

3. Design

Once the requirements have been defined, the project team moves on to designing the software. This stage involves creating a high-level and detailed design of the software architecture, data structures, user interface, and other components. This design will serve as a blueprint for the development team and ensure the product's scalability, maintainability, and extensibility.

4. Development

This is the stage where the actual coding takes place. The development team uses the design specifications to write code and build the software product. It is essential to follow coding standards and methodologies to ensure consistency and code quality. Regular code reviews and testing also take place during this stage to catch and fix any bugs or defects.

5. Testing

The testing stage involves checking the software for errors, bugs, and functionality issues. This ensures that the product is functioning as intended and meets the user's expectations. Various types of testing, such as unit testing, integration testing, and user acceptance testing, are performed at this stage to identify and rectify any issues.

6. Deployment

Once the software has been thoroughly tested and approved, it is ready for deployment. This involves installing and configuring the software on the intended devices and environments. The deployment process is closely monitored to ensure that everything is working correctly, and any issues are addressed promptly.

7. Maintenance

Software development does not end with the deployment of the product. The software will require regular maintenance to fix bugs, make updates, and add new features. This stage involves continuous improvement and support of the product to ensure its longevity and user satisfaction.

Best Practices

To ensure a successful software development project, it is crucial to follow certain best practices throughout the SDLC. These practices include:

Clear Communication

Communication is key in any team-based project, and software development is no different. It is essential to have open and transparent communication between all team members to ensure that everyone is on the same page and working towards the same goal.

User Involvement

User involvement is crucial as it ensures that the end product meets the needs and expectations of its intended audience. Involving users in the design, testing, and feedback stages can help identify and address any issues or features that may have been overlooked.

Continuous Testing

Testing should not be limited to the testing stage but should be an ongoing process throughout all stages of the SDLC. This helps catch and fix any issues earlier on, saving time and resources in the long run.

Version Control

Version control is crucial in software development as it helps track changes, maintain code quality, and allow for collaboration among team members. It also provides a backup of previous versions, ensuring that the project can be reverted to a previous state if needed.

Common Challenges

Software development is a complex and ever-changing process, and as such, it is not without its challenges. Some of the common challenges faced during the SDLC are:

Changing Requirements

User needs and expectations may change, leading to changing requirements throughout the development process. This can result in delays and budget overruns if not managed properly.

Technical Issues

Technical issues such as software compatibility, server crashes, and hardware failures can cause significant setbacks in the development process. It is crucial to have contingency plans in place to tackle these issues promptly.

Resource Management

Effective resource management is essential in software development. This includes managing time, budget, and team members' workload to ensure that the project stays on track and is completed within the allocated resources.

Scope Creep

It is common for a project's scope to increase beyond its initial boundaries, resulting in scope creep. This can lead to delays, bloated budgets, and an end product that does not meet the initial requirements.

In conclusion, the Software Development Life Cycle is a crucial process in software engineering that ensures the successful delivery of high-quality software products. By following best practices and addressing common challenges, development teams can streamline their processes and produce exceptional software that meets user needs and expectations.

Chapter 47: Project Management Tools

As software engineering has evolved, so has the complexity of projects. Gone are the days when a small team of developers could work on a project and manage everything themselves. With the growth of technology and globalization, projects have become more complex and teams have become larger. This has led to the need for effective project management tools to help teams stay organized, collaborate efficiently, and meet project deadlines. In this chapter, we will delve into the world of project management tools and how they have revolutionized the way software development projects are managed.

Introduction

Before the advent of project management tools, project management was a tedious and time-consuming process. Teams would have to rely on spreadsheets, emails, and other manual tools to track tasks, assign responsibilities, and communicate progress. This not only led to inefficiencies but also made it difficult to get a clear overview of the project. However, with the emergence of project management tools, this process has become much simpler and more streamlined.

Explanation

Project management tools are software applications designed to help teams plan, organize, and manage tasks and resources for a project. These tools provide a centralized platform for teams to collaborate, track progress, and communicate effectively. They offer a wide range of features, from task lists and time tracking to budget management and reporting. The use of project management tools has become essential for project success, as they help teams stay on top of tasks, identify potential issues, and make timely decisions.

Types

There are various types of project management tools available in the market. Some are general-purpose tools that can be used for any type of project, while others are designed for specific industries or project methodologies. The most common types of project management tools include:

- Task Management Tools: These are tools that help teams track individual tasks, set deadlines, assign responsibilities, and monitor progress.

- Time Tracking Tools: These tools allow teams to track the time spent on each task. This information is useful for analyzing productivity, identifying bottlenecks, and making adjustments to improve efficiency.

- Collaboration Tools: These tools provide a platform for teams to communicate and share files, as well as assign and manage tasks.

- Project Planning Tools: These tools are used for creating project plans, setting milestones, and monitoring project progress.

- Reporting Tools: These are tools that help teams generate reports and analyze project data, such as budget, schedule, and progress.

Depending on the specific needs of a project, teams may choose to use one or more of these types of project management tools.

Features

Project management tools come with a wide range of features to help teams manage projects effectively. Some of the common features include:

- Task List: This feature allows teams to create and assign tasks, set deadlines, and track progress.

- Collaboration: Most project management tools come with collaboration features, such as chat, file sharing, and commenting, to facilitate communication within the team.

- Gantt Charts: Gantt charts are visual representations of project schedules and timelines. They help teams identify dependencies and track the progress of various tasks.

- Time Tracking: This feature allows teams to track the time spent on each task, making it easier to analyze productivity and identify areas for improvement.

- Budget Management: Some project management tools come with features to track project expenses and manage budgets.

- Reporting: Reporting tools provide teams with insights into project progress and help identify any potential issues.

While these are some of the common features, project management tools often come with other features as well, depending on the type of tool and its intended use.

Conclusion

Project management tools have become an integral part of software development projects. They have revolutionized the way teams manage their tasks and resources, leading to more efficient and effective project management. With an ever-increasing range of features and types of tools available, teams can now choose the best project management tool to suit their specific project needs. With the help of these tools, project management has become more organized, transparent, and ultimately, more successful.

Chapter 48: Quality Assurance

Quality assurance is a crucial aspect of software engineering that ensures the final product meets the desired standards. It involves a systematic process of monitoring and evaluating the software's development to identify and address any flaws or issues before the product is released to the market. In this chapter, we will delve into the methods, tools, and importance of quality assurance in software engineering.

Methods

The primary goal of quality assurance is to improve the quality and reliability of the software. There are various methods used to achieve this, and one of the most commonly used is testing. Testing involves executing the software to identify any defects or bugs in its functionality. It is essential to have a well-defined testing strategy, including unit testing, integration testing, and system testing, to ensure comprehensive coverage. Another method used in quality assurance is code review. Code reviews involve a team of developers going through the software's code to identify any potential issues and provide feedback to improve its quality. This process not only helps catch errors but also promotes knowledge sharing and collaboration among team members.Documentation is also a critical method in quality assurance. Having well-documented processes and procedures can help improve the software's overall quality by providing clear guidelines and instructions for developers to follow. It also helps with maintaining the software in the long run, as new team members can easily understand and work with the code.

Tools

In addition to using various methods, there are also several quality assurance tools available to aid in the process. These tools range from code analysis tools to automated testing tools and can greatly improve the efficiency and effectiveness of quality assurance. Code analysis tools, like linters and static code analyzers, help identify potential issues in the code, such as syntax errors and coding standards violations. They can also provide suggestions for improving the code's quality, such as suggesting more efficient ways to write code or identifying potential security vulnerabilities. Automated testing tools are also widely used in quality assurance. These tools can automate various types of testing, such as unit testing, integration testing, and regression testing. They can significantly reduce the time and effort required for testing and can also help catch errors that may have been missed in manual testing.Collaboration tools, such as project management software and version control systems, also play a crucial role in quality assurance. They allow team members to work together seamlessly, track changes, and provide valuable insights into the project's progress.

Importance

Quality assurance is not just about ensuring the software meets specific standards; it also has a significant impact on the overall success of a software project. Quality assurance helps identify and address issues early in the development process, reducing the cost and effort required to fix them later on. By catching and addressing defects early on, quality assurance also helps improve the software's stability and reliability. This can lead to increased customer satisfaction and trust in the product, which can ultimately result in higher sales and revenue. Moreover, quality assurance promotes continuous improvement and learning within the development team. With regular code reviews, testing, and documentation, the team can identify areas for improvement and work together to implement them, resulting in better code quality and more efficient development processes. In addition to these benefits, quality assurance also plays a crucial role in maintaining the software in the long run. By documenting processes and procedures and continuously reviewing and improving the code, the software can remain stable and reliable, even as it evolves and expands over time.

In conclusion, quality assurance is a vital aspect of software engineering that cannot be overlooked. It provides a systematic approach to ensuring the final product meets desired standards and has numerous benefits for the overall success of a software project. By utilizing various methods and tools and understanding the importance of quality assurance, software engineering teams can produce high-quality, reliable, and successful products.

Chapter 49: User Experience Design

Definition

User Experience Design (UX Design) is the process of creating products or services that provide meaningful and relevant experiences to users. It involves understanding the needs, wants, and behaviors of the users and using that knowledge to design products that are intuitive, easy to use, and enjoyable.

Process

The process of User Experience Design starts with research and understanding the target audience. This involves conducting user interviews, surveys, and analyzing data to gain insights into the users' needs and preferences. Once the research phase is complete, the UX designer moves on to creating wireframes, prototypes, and user flows to visualize the product and test its usability.The next step is to refine the design based on feedback and iterate until the final product meets the users' needs and expectations. Additionally, the UX designer collaborates with cross-functional teams such as developers, product managers, and marketers to ensure that the product meets business goals while also delivering a great user experience.

Importance in Software Development

In today's digital age, where users have endless options and short attention spans, user experience design has become a crucial aspect of software development. A poor user experience can lead to user frustration, decreased engagement, and ultimately, diminished trust in the product or brand. On the other hand, a well-designed user experience can greatly influence user satisfaction, brand loyalty, and even profitability. When a product is designed with the user in mind, it becomes more intuitive and enjoyable to use, leading to higher user retention and customer satisfaction. User experience design also plays a significant role in differentiating a product from its competitors. In a crowded market, having a well-designed user experience can be the key factor in attracting and retaining users. Moreover, user experience design goes beyond just creating an aesthetically pleasing product. It also takes into consideration the user's emotions, motivations, and goals, resulting in a more human-centered design. By understanding the user's perspective, UX designers can create products that are not just useful but also meaningful and impactful. In software development, user experience design is not a one-time process but an ongoing one. As technology and user preferences continuously evolve, so do the design needs. Therefore, it is essential to have a UX design process in place to continuously improve and enhance the user experience of a product.

In conclusion, User Experience Design is a critical aspect of software development that focuses on creating products or services that provide exceptional user experiences. By understanding the needs, emotions, and behaviors of users, UX designers can create intuitive, enjoyable, and impactful products that stand out in the market. With the constant evolution of technology and user preferences, the importance of User Experience Design will only continue to grow in the software engineering industry.